SCHOOLYARD *Science*

SCHOOLYARD Science

101 EASY AND INEXPENSIVE ACTIVITIES

By Thomas R. Lord and Holly J. Travis

National Science Teachers Association

Arlington, Virginia

National Science Teachers Association

Claire Reinburg, Director
Jennifer Horak, Managing Editor
Andrew Cooke, Senior Editor
Judy Cusick, Senior Editor
Wendy Rubin, Associate Editor
Amy America, Book Acquisitions Coordinator

ART AND DESIGN
Will Thomas Jr., Director
Illustrations by Linda Olliver
Photos courtesy of iStockphoto

PRINTING AND PRODUCTION
Catherine Lorrain, Director

NATIONAL SCIENCE TEACHERS ASSOCIATION
Francis Q. Eberle, PhD, Executive Director
David Beacom, Publisher

Library of Congress Cataloging-in-Publication Data
Lord, Thomas R.
  Schoolyard science : 101 easy and inexpensive activities / by Thomas R. Lord and Holly J. Travis.
      p. cm.
  Includes bibliographical references and index.
  ISBN 978-1-936137-16-9
  1. Science--Study and teaching--Activity programs. I. Travis, Holly J. II. Title.
  LB1585.L58 2011
  372.35'044--dc22
                              2011004597

eISBN 978-1-936137-46-6

NSTA is committed to publishing material that promotes the best in inquiry-based science education. However, conditions of actual use may vary, and the safety procedures and practices described in this book are intended to serve only as a guide. Additional precautionary measures may be required. NSTA and the authors do not warrant or represent that the procedures and practices in this book meet any safety code or standard of federal, state, or local regulations. NSTA and the authors disclaim any liability for personal injury or damage to property arising out of or relating to the use of this book, including any of the recommendations, instructions, or materials contained therein.

SCI LINKS. *Featuring SciLinks—a new way of connecting text and the Internet. Up-to-the minute online content, classroom ideas, and other materials are just a click away. For more information, go to* www.scilinks. org/Faq.aspx.

CONTENTS

Chapter 6: Schoolyard Gardens and Nature Areas 49

Chapter 7: Insects and Other Invertebrates 65

Chapter 8: Studying Vertebrates 81

Chapter 9: Experimenting With How Animals Work.................................. 97

Chapter 10: Exploring Energy 107

Chapter 11: Earth Science 115

Preface

Change in societal values is similar to environmental change: Both happen slowly but constantly over time. Who could have predicted that we would be able to call friends miles away with a tiny phone we carry with us or that we would have miniature boxes in our pockets that play music, calculate equations, and keep a grocery list? While these technological advances are miraculous, they are not without their disadvantages. Store clerks can no longer make change without their computers, people become quickly frustrated when information is not available instantaneously, and children do not play outdoors as much as they used to.

With continued advances in electronic technologies over the decades, people of all ages are spending more of their time working and playing in front of a computer and less time enjoying the outdoors. Correlating with these disturbing trends, rising rates of obesity, hyperactivity, and stress, as well as general health problems, have affected our society. Mounting evidence points to the need for children and young adults to be reintroduced to nature. If the studies are correct, the nation's teachers will become instrumental in reversing these disturbing trends away from nature. Education associations throughout the nation have begun to rally behind the idea that schools can help improve the situation, and these groups are encouraging teachers to use the outdoors as much as possible when teaching their classes. Teachers in elementary, middle, and senior high schools are eager to respond but often are unable to find accessible information to help them in this critical endeavor, especially with dwindling funding and resources.

The ideas presented in this book are designed to give teachers an incentive to use the environment around their school in science lessons. The activities have been piloted with various students in classrooms, youth camp programs, and science education classes in teacher preparation programs. We are certainly cognizant of the obstacles that must be surmounted when taking students to natural environments, such as woodlands, parks, and environmental learning centers, which are located away from the school property. We have therefore designed this book to be used in outdoor sites on the school grounds.

We also designed this book for teachers who have limited background in scientific nomenclature. Names of plants and animals or anatomical structures they possess are not necessary for teachers to use this book effectively. Instead, the intent of this book is for students to develop observation skills and an appreciation for the environment, and for teachers to feel comfortable using natural resources available in the schoolyard. All activities align with one or more of the National Science Education Standards, use student-centered inquiry in their approach, and are noncompetitive. Finally, all activities in this book are developed around easily obtained and inexpensive materials.

This book focuses on teamwork, with most activities using teams composed of students of different genders and ability levels. The challenges presented to the student teams involve observing, constructing, or locating items in general ways. For example, students find five different types of red flowers; when the class has accomplished this task, teams come up with three advantages this color might confer on the plant that bears the flowers. The importance of these kinds of questions lies not in having the correct answers, but rather in improving students' critical-thinking skills and ability to work as a team to find the answers. Sharing results with other students is also an important goal of this type of teaching. (A list of references that discuss the importance of inquiry and student-centered learning can be found at the end of this book.)

Appropriate grade levels are included with each activity, but these are only guides. Any of these activities can be adapted to work with older or younger students. In addition, we have included a list of unusual or unique materials required for each activity. Please note that common materials such as pencils and paper are not listed because most classrooms have access to these items.

We hope this book will inspire teachers not only to use the activities described throughout but also to design additional activities and projects that build on the skills students develop as they spend time outside. No matter what age group teachers work with, they will find the activities in this book appealing and useful for young science students.

Acknowledgments

The authors would like to acknowledge the hundreds of science education majors at Indiana University of Pennsylvania over the past decade who gave suggestions and encouragement and helped pilot the activities in this book. It is through their persuasive support and insightful ideas that this book was conceived and developed.

About the Authors

After obtaining his doctorate degree from Rutgers University, **Tom Lord** began teaching at postsecondary institutions in and around Philadelphia; he eventually settled down at Indiana University of Pennsylvania, where he currently teaches biology and science education courses to undergraduate and graduate students. A disciple of open-ended inquiry instruction, Tom was presented with the Distinguished Educator Award at the university and earned recognition for Innovative Instruction and Pedagogical Research by the Center for Teaching Excellence. He was also honored with the Outstanding Researcher/Educator award from the National Association of Biology Teachers (NABT). Active in his profession, Tom has presented dozens of talks, seminars, symposia, and panels at national professional meetings and has directed several half-day and daylong science workshops at NABT and NSTA, as well as the NSF-sponsored Chautauqua short course program. He has written more than 100 peer-reviewed science and science education articles in reputable journals, 2 monographs, and 5 books on science and science education topics; he has also contributed chapters to several books.

Tom has just completed a two-year term as president of the Society for College Science Teachers, where he wrote a monthly column in the *Journal for College Science Teaching*. Over that time, he also served on the Alliance of Affiliates of NSTA Executive Board and was on the *JCST* editorial advisory board. Not yet ready to retire, Tom recently accepted the challenge of the office of president of the Four Year College Division of NABT.

Holly Travis is a faculty member in the biology department at Indiana University of Pennsylvania, where she teaches biology and science education courses and coordinates the biology education program. She shares her office with numerous insects, arthropods, and reptiles, including Madagascar hissing cockroaches, African giant black millipedes, several species of stick insects, and assorted lizards and snakes. Throughout the year, Dr. Travis works with a variety of school and camp programs, including the Junior Naturalist Outdoor Adventure Camps and Crooked Creek Environmental Learning Center, to share her collection of critters and love of the outdoors. She was the recipient of the Armstrong Conservation District Outstanding Educator Award in 2008. Dr. Travis also serves as the science coordinator for the IUP Upward Bound Math and Science Program, where she is responsible for the design and implementation of science programming, including content, research opportunities, associated writing and mathematics skills, and field activities for

30–50 Indiana County high school students in grades 9–12. In addition, she serves on numerous college and university committees for assessment and teacher education.

Dr. Travis has presented dozens of talks and seminars at local, state, and national professional meetings; published several peer-reviewed science and science education articles; and contributed chapters to two monographs. She is a co-author of two books and serves as a reviewer for both science and education journals. In addition, she serves as the coordinator for the Jefferson County (PA) Animal Response Team and is a frequent volunteer for Groundhog Day activities in her hometown of Punxsutawney, PA.

1 Introduction

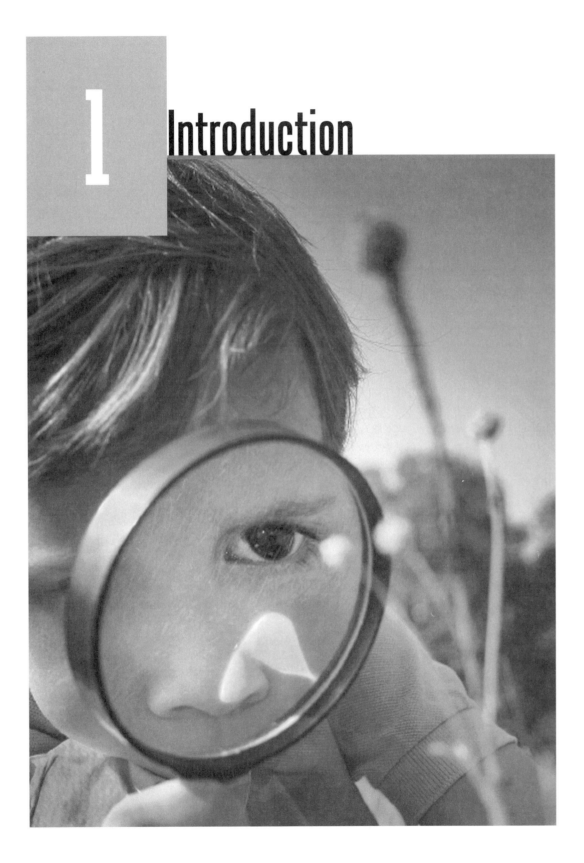

Inquiry in Science Education

In 1983 the National Commission on Excellence in Education (NCEE), initiated by then-President Reagan, released its findings on the state of education in America's schools. The document, *A Nation at Risk*, presented the United States with a wake-up call concerning the deterioration of learning in America's youth (NCEE 1983). The study found that our students' gains in knowledge are not keeping up with children of equal ages in other developed countries. Distressed by the report, the federal government increased the financial commitment to education, which led to further research on student learning and the teaching methods used to educate children. Despite these efforts, student learning assessments have found that not much has changed in the past 30 years. Children in the United States today are not learning as much as U.S. students did three decades ago; students in other countries also learn more than U.S. students today.

One of the methods suggested by the research, however, did demonstrate pupils' learning gains—a philosophy called *constructivism*, which used the inquiry strategy for learning. With inquiry, students meet in small groups to discuss, plan, and develop solutions to questions. In this student-centered approach, open-ended questions designed by the teacher before the class replace a didactic description of the subject matter presented directly from the classroom teacher. By working together to direct the processes of science, students gain a deeper understanding of the information. Research shows that if a lasting increase in knowledge is to be obtained, understanding *how* science is truly done is as important as the actual content itself.

If teachers visit schools comparable to their own in other developed countries, the differences become very apparent. Rarely do students ask their teacher to tell them *what they need to know,* then become distraught if they are not told. Rarely does one see students verbally repeating descriptions of the content that the teacher has presented. The visitor sees students describing the content in their own words or using the content in a different way than it was provided by the teacher. When students can answer questions and apply information in their own words, rather than reciting facts verbatim, the teacher can be more or less assured that the student understands the content. The best teachers in this country also teach this way, but many instructors still rely on presenting what students need to know to pass the class.

Lectures and cookbook lab exercises, by themselves, rarely reach the level where students truly understand information. When students can recite content information, teachers accept this as proof that students know the material. When pressed on what they understand, many students either have no adequate explanation or provide a plausible but erroneous grasp of the material. Unfortunately, many teachers do not pursue the issue when this happens; lack of understanding and misconceptions are then perpetuated.

This complacency is common and troublesome to the nation's education. More teachers are relying on textbooks and laboratory books to direct learning. Publishers are happy to provide well-written materials with fancy, slick, colorful graphics. Unfortunately, contemporary textbook publishers are providing teachers with exactly *what they need to teach* for students to see *what they need to know to pass the course.* To carry it a step further, a side industry has developed in America where the materials needed to perform a particular exercise are packaged in shoe box–size containers and shipped to schools each week so each student group can do their lab. This service removes the client from getting involved in the learning. This has further instilled a "tell me what I need to know" attitude not only in students but in teachers as well.

About This Book

Closely following the inquiry model of open-ended question design, this book offers ideas that can be done easily outside the classroom. Set within general categories, numerous rich and fascinating environmental science activities that excite student learning and understanding are presented. Driven by current research that finds science learning is enriched for students when the learning takes place in a natural setting, the book describes activities that can be performed on the school grounds easily and inexpensively. By investigating science locally, student learning can take place without the need for parental permission slips, costly additional insurance, or expensive bus transportation.

This book is not a series of lessons that describe what a teacher must do. Rather, we provide a series of educationally rich suggestions and ideas that a teacher can adapt to create lessons in a manner compatible with his or her background and resources. A teacher might have to consult additional sources to brush up on background information or improvise an activity. However, teachers are adept at adapting others' suggestions based on their own research and needs; this process is what quality educators use to create novel, stimulating learning experiences for their students. The teacher also develops assessments for the activities. While some suggestions are offered throughout the book, the teacher will want to relate the assessments to his or her own standards and classroom needs based on how the teacher uses the activities. In this way, the authors hope that teachers are also developing skills and satisfying their own curiosity as they use this book, rather than following cookbook instructions and doing rote experiments.

For teachers who do not have much outdoor experience or background, we have included a list of resources at the end of this book. These books and websites are an excellent starting point. Information about plants, insects, and animals in the area around the school is also available through state and local extension agencies. These agencies often provide guest speakers and lists of local experts in various topics for educational programs.

Two common assessment tools for outdoor activities, nature journals and field reports, are discussed below. These can be adapted for various age groups and activities but are certainly not the only way to evaluate student learning. Presentations, research reports, creative writing assignments, and models are among the options for teachers to assess student learning. Each teacher will determine what works best for his or her curriculum and learning goals.

Nature Journals

We recommend students work through activities from this book by keeping modest records of their experiences in a field book or journal. The nature journal should include observations, opinions, personal reflections, and sketches. Students also may include pressed leaves or flowers from an activity, stories or poems written about their experiences in the natural world, and other creative or informal assignments. One way to make the journals unique is to use the paper-making activity and have each student create a cover for his or her nature journal. Teachers might use the nature journals as a form of assessment by grading a specific entry, which could be another application of an observed concept or an explanation of the scientific processes involved in the activities that students completed.

Field Reports

Field reports are different from nature journals. Journals are written diaries of the field experiences, but field reports are accurate records taken at the site. Field reports generally include materials used and expected outcomes. Data such as the amount of rainfall that fell during the lab or the fluctuations in temperature over the work session would also be recorded. What sampling was done and any data that were collected should be part of the report, along with specific items discovered and measured. From the information recorded in the reports, students draw conclusions, discuss outcomes, and plot or graph results.

Please note that science should not be done in isolation from other key subject areas. Integrating creative writing, descriptive writing, oral and visual presentations, measuring, counting, or graphing as a part of the lesson (see Tables 1.1 and 1.2 [p. 6]) not only helps create varied assessments of student learning but also makes it easier to find time to do science activities while not taking away from other key content areas.

How to Use These Ideas

Because the ideas in this book are not designed as step-by-step lesson plans, we offer two examples of how these activities might be incorporated into the classroom curriculum. The lessons found in Tables 1.1 and 1.2 are presented using the 5E Instructional Model of lesson plan development, first described by Trowbridge and Bybee (1990), because this model makes it easy to create student-centered lessons that focus on questioning and inquiry. The examples in Tables 1.1 and 1.2 are based on Activity 36, Seed Dispersal Techniques (p. 43), and show how a single idea from this book can be adapted for various ages and classroom needs.

Practical Fieldwork Considerations

Keeping the materials needed for an activity close at hand makes the time spent outside more productive and less stressful for both the teacher and the students. It is also faster and easier to collect all the equipment at the end of the activity if everyone knows where to put all of the items. For this reason, field containers and field bags should be used.

Table 1.1.

5E Description and Sample preK–3 Grade-Level Lesson Based on Activity 36, Seed Dispersal Techniques (p. 43)

	Description	Example
Engage	A brief activity, question, demonstration, or film "snippet" that whets the students' appetites and focuses their attention on the topic	Bring in a dandelion that has gone to seed and ask students what happens when they blow on it or when the wind blows. If dandelions are not available, substitute a brief film clip showing the same thing (e.g., *www. youtube.com/watch?v=u8_gDqZGSq4*).
Explore	An activity in which the students develop questions and attempt to answer them, or challenge questions that encourage the students to think in depth about the topic	Once the class is outside, ask students to work in small groups to locate five different types of seeds from flowers, trees, and shrubs in the schoolyard. When they have collected the seeds, have students determine how the seeds are likely to move around. You might offer suggestions as necessary, including wind, animal fur, and water, or as a food source.
Explain	Groups share their results, whether they have done an experiment or worked through a question. At this point, the teacher can also clear up misconceptions and misinformation to ensure that students understand the material.	Groups will share their seeds and dispersal ideas with the rest of the class. Have students compare the similarities and differences of the seeds collected. Throughout this discussion, the teacher will clarify ideas and clear up misconceptions about what is or is not a seed, how seeds move, and so on.
Elaborate	Groups might do further laboratory work, do research, give presentations, or simply discuss more complex questions within their groups, allowing them to build a deeper understanding and to relate this information to other material covered in class.	Have each group (or each student) design a seed. They can use paper, string, glue, crayons, and other craft supplies. Older students might be given a pumpkin or sunflower seed and asked to devise a new "pod" to help it spread to other areas. Take the models outside to see how they work. In their nature journals (if age-appropriate), each student can write an entry describing his or her seed and dispersal method. They can also include what they might change after their trials.
Evaluate	Evaluation can take numerous forms, including standard quizzes or tests, written assignments, oral presentations, student self-evaluations, or observation of student participation in group activities.	Have students do a creative writing assignment in which they describe the life of the seed, how its structure helps it move from place to place, and what the seed might observe as it moves to a new germination spot. Younger children can draw a picture showing where their seed ends up or what it looks like when it becomes a plant. Close the lesson by reading a book such as *The Tiny Seed* by Eric Carle or *A Dandelions's Life* by John Himmelman (see Resources on p. 127 for publication information).

Table 1.2.

5E Description and Sample 4–8 Grade-Level Lesson Based on Activity 36, Seed Dispersal Techniques (p. 43)

	Description	Example
Engage	A brief activity, question, demonstration, or film snippet that whets the students' appetites and focuses their attention on the topic	Show a brief video clip of seed dispersal, such as *www.youtube.com/watch?v=u8_gDqZGSq4*. Ask students (or groups of students) to list at least six different kinds of seeds. For each seed, have students describe how it is dispersed. Have groups share the example they feel is most unusual.
Explore	An activity in which the students develop questions and attempt to answer them, or challenge questions that encourage the students to think in depth about the topic	Take student groups outside and ask each group to find 10 different seeds. Determine the dispersal mechanism for each, and evaluate the effectiveness by counting the number of each kind of seed students find and the average distance from the parent plant. They may need to use field guides to identify the parent plant for each seed. (The Peterson and Audubon Field Guides [listed in Additional Resources on p. 128] include pictures of seeds or fruits from many common plants.). If necessary, include time to research their seeds online or in the library.
Explain	Groups share their results, whether they have done an experiment or worked through a question. At this point, the teacher can also clear up misconceptions and misinformation to ensure that students understand the material.	Have each group share their results, looking at which seeds were moved farthest away from the parent plant. Have students offer suggestions about which characteristics seemed to be most effective and which ones did not work as well for seed dispersal.
Elaborate	Groups might do further laboratory work, do research, give presentations, or simply discuss more complex questions within their groups, allowing them to build a deeper understanding and to relate this information to other material covered in class.	Groups will choose one type of plant and design a research project to test their observations from the Explore activity. It may be most effective to use those that are wind-dispersed, but that can be left up to the teacher, based on what students find in the schoolyard. These research projects will include a hypothesis, experimental design, data collection and analysis, and conclusions. Have the groups carry out the research projects to check their hypotheses.
Evaluate	Evaluation can take numerous forms, including standard quizzes or tests, written assignments, oral presentations, student self-evaluations, or observation of student participation in group activities.	Students will write a formal lab report using the data they collected and graphing results. Conclusions should include discussion of how the adaptations of that plant improve the effectiveness of seed dispersal and a critique of the experimental design used, including changes that could be made to improve the accuracy of their results.

Field Containers

We encourage teachers to establish a container that holds common materials students will need for their investigations. This may be a large cloth bag, a plastic storage box or tote, or a laundry basket. It should be sturdy, easily portable, and large enough to hold several basic items that will be used frequently as students explore the schoolyard environment. These items may include magnifying glasses, scissors, rulers, various plastic containers, string, and pencils that can be taken into the schoolyard on the days the students work there. The container can also hold any field guides or other reference materials students will use as they observe plants and animals in the area. A basic first-aid kit should also be included so it is readily available if needed.

Field Bags

Each student or team should have a small bag that will hold the essential items for the activity they will be doing on any given day. For example, students may need magnifying glasses, rulers or measuring tape, notebook paper, and pencils one day. They may need safety goggles, vinyl gloves, plastic bags, identification guides, and thermometers another day. Students can easily keep track of their supplies if they have a handy place to keep them while they are outside.

Some Notes on Outdoor Safety

Concerns about safety should not prevent teachers and students from spending time outdoors, but using common sense and some simple guidelines will ensure that the activities are enjoyable for everyone. Teachers should always consider their students' ages and the teaching environment when determining what safety precautions are necessary. The following list, taken in part from *Exploring Safely: A Guide for Elementary Teachers* (Kwan and Texley 2002) and *Inquiring Safely: A Guide for Middle School Teachers* (Kwan and Texley 2003), provides some basic considerations. These can be adapted to fit your school and class requirements. These guidelines will not all apply to all the activities identified in this book, and some additional safety precautions have been noted in specific instances.

1. Link field trips and field studies to curriculum goals.
2. Preview the site and abutting properties before planning your field study.
3. Determine proper clothing and footwear for the site and activities planned. (Please note that this might include vinyl gloves, aprons, and protective eyewear, as noted in several of the activities.)
4. Meet with cooperating resource people to plan activities.
5. Orient and train all chaperones in your planned activities and in safety precautions.
6. Review Material Safety Data Sheets (MSDS) for any chemicals that will be used and use appropriate safety precautions.
7. Always have students wash their hands thoroughly with soap and water after doing outside activities, especially those involving animals, soils, and water.

8. Consider student allergies (peanut butter, latex, bee stings, etc.) and medical conditions before doing activities that might trigger reactions.
9. Follow common safety rules that apply in and out of the classroom. These include, but are not limited to,

   - modeling proper use of equipment;
   - using only nonmercury thermometers;
   - reminding students to use equipment such as magnifying glasses, scissors, and knives in a safe manner; and
   - having additional adult supervision when warranted by the complexity of the activities or setting.

Final Thoughts From the Authors

It is essential for the health and well-being of both our children and our environment that we allow children to experience nature. Numerous studies have shown that spending time outside leads to healthier children, both physically and mentally. This book was designed to provide ideas that allow teachers to do exactly that, without the need for complex equipment and extensive funding. These activities are offered as a starting point, and teachers can mold and adapt them as necessary to meet varied curriculum needs and assessment goals. As any teacher knows, additional work will be involved in developing these ideas into lessons that are appropriate for a particular class in a particular location. The internet offers many resources that allow teachers to access quickly and easily the background information they need to feel confident with their students.[*] Libraries will have books and field guides that can provide expertise. These lessons are also a great way to involve community experts who can work with students on a special topic or project. The most important objective of this book is to keep teachers and students actively learning and spending time outside in the natural world.

References

Kwan, T., and Texley, J. 2002. *Exploring safely: A guide for elementary teachers.* Arlington, VA: NSTA Press.

Kwan, T., and Texley, J. 2003. *Inquiring safely: A guide for middle school teachers.* Arlington, VA: NSTA Press.

National Commission on Excellence in Education (NCEE). 1983. *A nation at risk: The imperative for educational reform.* Washington, DC: U.S. Government Printing Office.

Trowbridge, L., and R. Bybee. 1990. *Becoming a secondary school science teacher.* 5th ed. Englewood Cliffs, NJ: Merrill.

---

[*] An Additional Resources section on page 128 can be used as a starting point when looking for information for both teachers and students.

2 Introduction to Nature

Activity 1. Exploring the Human Senses in Nature (preK–8)

NSES Science Content Standards

- Unifying concepts and processes in science
- Science as inquiry
- Life science
- Science in personal and social perspectives

Additional materials: jars with lids (1c), small paper bags (1b, 1d, 1h)

Topic: The Senses
Go to: *www.scilinks.org*
Code: SYS001

Most students can recall the pleasant smell of flowers or the awful smell of rotting garbage. Some can remember the fresh smell of the air after a thunderstorm and the frightening sound of thunder that accompanies the storm. We use our senses continuously during the day, much of the time in such subtle ways that we are not cognizant of their presence. To encourage students to recognize how important the five senses are to their everyday lives, have the class sit quietly in the schoolyard for a brief time and list in their nature journal what senses they experience. While texts often suggest students will experience five senses (sight, smell, hearing, taste, and touch) when quietly experiencing nature, they will actually come up with many more sensing experiences. They will feel the breeze pass through their hair and the pain of a pebble in their shoes. They will feel the heat of the Sun on their faces and the cool skin on the back of their necks. They may sense an air pressure increase when the wind picks up, and they will experience weight on their knees folded under their bodies. Students enjoy this experience in a special way, for it incorporates many of the same principles as meditation.

a. Sensory hike (preK–3)

A more active offshoot of the above activity is to have students discuss the senses they are experiencing with each other as they walk around the school grounds. This activity is generally preferred by teachers of younger children.

b. Identifying natural objects when hidden from view (preK–3)

In this fun activity, students collect in a small bag items from a walk. The next day, they use their senses to identify the objects when they are blindfolded or when the item is placed in a sock. Students can use any sense *except* sight and taste (i.e., touch, smell, hearing) to identify the item.

c. Capturing smells in a jar (preK–3)

Believe it or not, a person can capture smells in a jar! Air from a specific location holds odor molecules from various items in that specific region. Scent molecules from flowers, grasses, soils, and water are continuously released into the air and can be captured in a jar for a short period of time. This is particularly noticeable in still air or freshened (ozone-rich) air after a thunderstorm. Have groups capture air from various parts of the school-yard in a medium-size jar, such as a mayonnaise jar, and rendezvous with other groups to share the smells they have collected.

d. Identifying flowers and fruits by their smells (preK–3)

This activity is similar to the capturing smells exercise above, but this time student teams locate 10 different kinds of flowers or 10 different kinds of fruits in the schoolyard and place each in a separate paper lunch bag. After a short time, the teams return to a location and present their findings to another team. Challenge each team to identify the 10 fruits or flowers gathered by another team by using only a sense of smell.

e. What is that sound? (preK–8)

There are many ways to experience how much sound impacts our lives. For example, we can hear a sound somewhere around the school and determine where it came from and what created it (e.g., chatter of a squirrel or chipmunk, warning calls of birds, hoot of an owl). Students come up with a variety of opinions for what made one sound.

f. Draw what is described. (preK–8)

Another way to compare students' interpretations entails having one student describe something he or she has seen in and around the school but that is not visible. The remainder of the class attempts to draw what is being depicted without consulting other students. Students are surprised that most of their classmates do not draw the same thing.

g. Listen to nature. (preK–8)

Still another fun way to explore hearing is to have students identify items by the way they sound when wind blows through them. It is possible to distinguish large trees from small trees, as well as determine whether the wind is blowing through leafy or bare branches, if the wind is sending leaves into a whorl or blowing dust against a wall, or whether some-one or something is approaching.

h. Identifying natural objects by touch (preK–3)

Exploring the sense of touch can be very revealing. Tactile nerve endings in the fingers and palm respond to what is being felt and send impulses to the brain's parietal lobe for interpretation. A good way for students to realize the sensitivity of touch is to have them identify items without seeing them. Each team finds 10 small items (less than 2 in.) around the schoolyard and places them in a paper bag. Assemble the bags and redistribute them to different teams. Challenge the teams to identify all the items in the bag using only the sense of touch. *Caution students not to collect trash, sharp objects, moldy items, or other items that can cause harm.*

Activity 2. Animal Signs (preK–8)

NSES Science Content Standards

- Unifying concepts and processes in science
- Science as inquiry
- Life science
- Science in personal and social perspectives
- History and nature of science

Additional materials: animal silhouettes (2e), pictures of animal beaks, feet, eyes, skin, etc. (2f)

> Footprints, droppings, scents, skins, hair, feathers, cocoons, galls, nests, paths, scratch or rub marks, bones, chewed leaves, chewed bark, songs, chirps, growls, slime, shedding, corpuses, wallows, holes in trees, tail drag, and matted-down patches of grass are common animal signs.

Periodically, a student will spot a colorful feather or an animal footprint on the way to school, but numerous signs of animals throughout the environment go unnoticed. Students do not pay as much attention to their surroundings as children did a half century ago. Ask student teams to open their eyes to nature and try to locate eight different signals or signs left by animals in the schoolyard.

a. The stories that animal signs can tell (preK–8)

When animal signs are found together, it is fun to tell stories of events that could have taken place when the signs were created. For example, when large footprints are found *next to* the same type of small footprints, students could imagine that an adult and a young animal were walking next to one another. If a large set of footprints was found *behind* a small set of footprints from a different animal, however, students could imagine that the small animal was trying to escape the large one (and if the small series of footprints disappears but the large ones continue on, students could imagine that the large animal caught the small one). Challenge student teams to locate different animal signs near each other on the school grounds and come up with a story that might explain these signs.

b. Creating animal signs that can go with a story (preK–3)

Sometimes students cannot find animal signs to use to make up a story, especially if the weather has been hot and dry. To compensate, students can construct their own animal signs from modeling clay, cotton balls, stems, and leaves. After several minutes of making signs, students can find locations around the schoolyard to set up their animal signs in a pattern to tell a story. Allow students to visit each other's story site so the story creators can share their tales.

c. Animal acting (preK–3)

This is a great activity for young students who seem to especially enjoy playing pretend. Each student finds information on the habits and behavior of a specific animal found in the schoolyard. When it is time to go outdoors, students walk to a rendezvous site as quietly as they can so they do not scare the wild animals. At the site, each student demonstrates his or her animal without telling the others which animal they are imitating. When the student finishes acting, the other students guess what animal the student was pretending to be. Once the class has guessed the animal, each student can describe unique characteristics of his or her animal to classmates.

d. Animal stalking (preK–3)

Students generally love to sneak up on things. Some have learned that if they walk slowly, stepping on the outside of their feet and rolling them inward to the toes, they can walk silently. This takes practice, and in this activity they will see how difficult it can be. Challenge small groups of students to walk quietly like a cat or fox, and see how close they can get to a wild resident of the schoolyard (e.g., a squirrel, rabbit, or bird). *Caution students to stay a safe distance away from wild animals, and do not surround or corner them. Stay clear of animals exhibiting bizarre or unusual behavior.*

e. Identifying animal silhouettes (preK–3)

It is fun to try to identify wild animals by their shadows or silhouettes. The task can be made easy for younger students by selecting schoolyard animals that are not closely related (i.e., rabbits and skunks) or can be made more difficult for older students by selecting shadows of animals in the same family (e.g., different birds). Challenge students to try to identify most of the animal shadows the teacher presents.

f. Identifying animals by parts of their anatomy (4–8)

Most students can tell the difference between the foot of a duck and the foot of a deer, but when the animals are closely related (e.g., foot of a dog and foot of a cat), the task can be really challenging. This exercise can be done with impressions or pictures from animals that reside around the school or in habitats away from the school. When students have had some practice, try using animal eyes, bird beaks, frog patterns, and snake skins.

Activity 3. Camouflage in Nature (preK–8)

NSES Science Content Standards
* Unifying concepts and processes in science
* Science as inquiry
* Life science

Additional materials: assorted stuffed or plastic animals

Animals in nature are masters at using camouflage to aid their survival. Students can hunt for these organisms, taking pictures to share with classmates

SCI**LINKS**
THE WORLD'S A CLICK AWAY

Topic: Adaptations of Animals
Go to: *www.scilinks.org*
Code: SYS002

later. Each group can put together an "I Spy" type of game, letting other groups or even other classes in the school find the hidden animals.

- Find four examples of insect camouflage. Grasshoppers, several moth species, katydids, stick insects, and praying mantises are just a few examples of great camouflage found in insects. Have student groups look in different types of habitats around the school—such as grassy areas, leaf litter, on trees or in shrubs, or near flowers—to find a wider variety of examples. *Use caution in working around leaf litter or grassy areas—these may contain mold, ticks, and other health hazards.*

- Find four examples of animal camouflage. For younger children, you can set up a hide-and-seek game using various stuffed or plastic animals in natural and artificial colors. Hide the animals ahead of time and have students walk through the area, seeing how many stuffed animals they can find. By using some that blend in and some that stand out, students can see the value of camouflage for animal survival. Older students can look for real examples of animal camouflage. Lots of common animals that use camouflage—such as squirrels, chipmunks, and birds—can be spotted almost anywhere.

- Find four examples of predators using camouflage. Once students have had the chance to observe several examples of camouflage in nature, they can look at the different ways animals use their camouflage. Challenge students to find examples of predators that use their ability to blend in to catch their prey. How does this help the predators become better hunters?

- Find four examples of prey camouflage. On the flip side, how does camouflage help animals avoid being eaten? What are some ways that insects and animals of all types make themselves less obvious to predators?

Activity 4. Nature Walks (preK–8)

NSES Science Content Standards
- Unifying concepts and processes in science
- Life science
- Earth and space science
- Science and technology
- Science in personal and social perspectives
- History and nature of science

Topic: Seasons
Go to: *www.scilinks.org*
Code: SYS003

In all parts of the country, nature in the schoolyard changes through the seasons. In some regions, environmental fluctuations are subtle, the levels of wind and rain being the primary variations. In other regions, the changes are more obvious, as large fluctuations in temperature affect not only the winds and precipitation but also the plants and animals. Despite the apparent changes, many students are unaware of what is occurring around them and sometimes even within the schoolyard. Students should walk around the schoolyard in different seasons and identify the effects the changing climate has had on nature. For example, students may notice the changing colors of the leaves in northern states in autumn but tend not to see how the changing weather affects seed dispersal patterns or insect egg-laying. Students also may not be aware of such spring occurrences as territory establishment, variation in sunlight patterns, changes in wind patterns, accelerated herbaceous growth, and animal rearing patterns (particularly insects).

To improve their understanding of seasonal changes, students can collect objects in the schoolyard throughout the year and place what they find in different shoe boxes labeled with the season's name (e.g., autumn box, winter box) or develop a seasonal scrapbook comparing various items they collected (e.g., a maple leaf found in each of the seasons) throughout the year. By studying these changes, students can compare adaptations and unique characteristics of plants and animals.

Changes that occur over the seasons in the evening sky are also poorly understood by students. Activities that direct students' attention to seasonal patterns of stars are always well-received additions to a school's science program.

As an interesting alternative to the nature walk, students can take an *unnatural walk*. Sometimes it is beneficial for students to walk along a trail that has been grossly disturbed with cans, papers, and other junk. If needed, set up the trail ahead of time by strewing different types of litter along the sides or on a path. Challenge students to find as many examples of litter as they can as they walk from beginning to end. *Students should be cautioned not to touch or pick up litter without hand protection, such as vinyl gloves.*

Activity 5. Magnifying Nature Items (preK–8)

NSES Science Content Standards
- Science as inquiry
- Physical science
- Life science
- Science and technology

Additional materials: binoculars (5a), magnifying lenses (5b), telescopes (5c)

Students will enjoy seeing nature items they have never noticed by using binoculars, hand lenses, and telescopes to look at nature more closely.

a. Binoculars (preK–3)

Before going into the schoolyard, have students write a word or draw picture of a plant or animal on a 3 in. × 5 in. index card. The students bring their cards with them into the field and affix them to trees, signs, or playground equipment in the schoolyard. Move the class away from the cards and provide binoculars to as many students as possible (you might also consider asking the students to bring binoculars from home). Allow each student a chance to discover how to use the binoculars by having them locate and focus on the card they prepared beforehand. When all the students have successfully focused and observed with the binoculars, have them repeat the action by observing their classmates' cards. You might even place a mystery card or two that you have designed around the yard. Because identifying words is more difficult for students, you might break this activity into two parts, practicing first with pictures and then using words.

Observing closely related items on cards: To stimulate excitement about using binoculars, you can organize an identification walk using 3 in. × 5 in. index cards. For this activity, tack a series of different animals of the same family, such as birds, to trees along a walk around the school grounds (obscuring some with shrub branches) before the class begins. During class, have students keep track of the kinds and number of birds they spot on the trip and discuss them in their nature journals.

Observing live organisms: The fun part of this exercise is locating and observing living organisms such as birds, squirrels, and plants through the binoculars. It is surprising to see the concentration and time that students (particularly older ones) spend on this exercise.

b. Magnifying lenses (preK–3)

Looking at nearby objects through small, handheld magnifiers can be just as exciting for students as seeing distant objects through binoculars. Introduce the correct use of magnifiers by having students observe words in their nature journals or grains of soil held in their hands. Once students are comfortable with the magnifiers, they can explore nature by looking through the lenses at items around their school. Magnifying items such as the parts of flowers, mouthparts of insects, undersides of ferns, and the skin of earthworms will stir excitement in even the most disinterested students. *Remind students never to observe the Sun through a magnifying lens, as doing so can cause serious eye damage.*

c. Telescopes (preK–8)

If students hold two different-size magnifying glasses in line with one another at opposite ends of a cardboard cylinder, they will create a telescope. When students do this, they should have the smaller lens nearer their eye and the larger one farther out. Have them look toward the object they want to magnify on the school grounds, which likely will be out of focus. Move the magnifying glass closest to the eye forward or backward until the image comes into focus. The image will appear larger but upside-down. Have a second student measure the distance between the two lenses. Cut a slot using scissors or a knife in the cardboard roll about an inch from the end to hold the large magnifying glass (being careful not to cut the roll entirely in two). Now cut another slot for the small magnifying glass at the same distance as the in-focus image appeared (recorded in the nature journal by the second student). Secure the two lenses in their positions with tape and cut off the excess length of tube. The image that was viewed earlier should now be in clear focus.

The telescope can be modified to handle a variety of focus lengths by using two cardboard rolls, one a bit bigger than the other, so the smaller one fits inside the larger one. With the large magnifying glass at the end of one roll and the smaller one at the end of the other, the focus length can be adjusted for various objects simply by moving the two lenses closer together or farther apart in the sliding roll. *Remind students never to observe the Sun through a magnifying lens, as doing so can cause serious eye damage.*

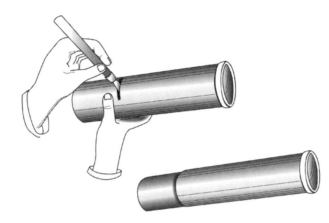

Activity 6. Weights and Measures (4–8)

NSES Science Content Standards
- Unifying concepts and processes in science
- Physical science
- Earth and space science
- Science and technology

SC*L*INKS.
THE WORLD'S A CLICK AWAY

Topic: Ways to Measure
Go to: *www.scilinks.org*
Code: SYS004

Additional materials: standard weights (6a), balance scale (6a), glass jars with lids (6c), straws (6c), clay (6c), food coloring (6c)

Most students have seen and used scales to weigh objects, including themselves. Many do not understand the idea behind standard weights or the difference between weight and density until they have a chance to examine these properties themselves.

a. Standard masses/density demonstration (4–8)
Students should fill bottles with appropriate amounts of water or sand found around the schoolyard to make a standard mass for use on a simple balance scale. This will familiarize students with different mass amounts. Bottles filled with different substances—such as rice, water, or sand—will demonstrate the concept of density; filling bottles with different

substances so they have the same mass but different volumes provides another a way to demonstrate density. Encourage students to make predictions about which substances will have similar or very different masses.

b. Making a simple seesaw balance (4–8)

Once students have created a common weight such as 1 oz., 1 lb., or 5 lbs. in their bottles (as described previously), they can design a simple balance with a flat piece of wood or bark and a rounded rock as the fulcrum. They can find natural items that have the same weight as the standard bottles they created in the previous exercise, such as leaves, twigs, pebbles, or grass. See if they can weigh 1 oz. or 1 lb. of dandelions or other flower seeds. Challenge groups to find the most dense or least dense natural items.

c. Making a simple thermometer (4–8)

Students can also make a thermometer that will measure temperatures between 32 and 212°F (or between 0 and 100°C). Participants need a glass jar with a tight-fitting lid; a long, thin drinking straw; clay; food coloring; and cold water. First, you or the students should make a hole in the lid of the jar as close to the diameter of the straw as possible using a nail or drill. Next, students insert the end of the straw in the lid and seal it tightly with clay. They then completely fill the bottle to the top with very cold water (no ice). Students screw the lid on, place it in the sunshine on the school grounds, and watch what happens as the water warms up, checking the height of the water in the straw every hour or so. As the temperature increases, the water expands and moves up the straw. To make this happen more quickly, students can place the jar full of cold water into a pan of hot water. *Teachers should make the hole in the lid or closely supervise students to avoid injury. Be careful with water, as water above 120°F may cause burns.*

Activity 7. Biodiversity Activities Within a Small Area on the School Grounds (preK–3)

NSES Science Content Standards
- Unifying concepts and processes in science
- Science as inquiry
- Life science

Students enjoy finding new things in an outdoor environment and are often surprised by the number of different organisms they can observe in a small area. In this activity, student teams check for different natural items within a plastic hoop or string circle. Some items students find on the school grounds include different shapes and types of leaves, different kinds of invertebrates, different types of soil particles, or different kinds and colors of flowers. Comparing, counting, and sorting are all skills that students can develop through these activities.

Activity 8. Biodiversity Activities in a Larger Tree or Shrub Area on the School Grounds (preK–8)

NSES Science Content Standards
- Unifying concepts and processes in science
- Science as inquiry
- Life science

Topic: Biodiversity
Go to: *www.scilinks.org*
Code: SYS005

When students search through a large area of the school grounds, they greatly expand the variety of items located. Some of the items they commonly find include different kinds of shrub or tree branches; different kinds, shapes, colors, and vein patterns of tree leaves; different types and patterns of tree bark; different types, colors, buds, and thorns on stems; different types of lichen, fungi, or algae on tree bark; different types of grasses, mosses, and ferns; different types of seeds, fruits, and cones; different types, shapes, and colors of flowers; different arrangements of flower components, different indications (tracks, droppings, or shelters) of animals; or different indications of erosion. *Caution students not to pick up animal droppings.*

Activity 9. Biodiversity in a Rotting Log (4–8)

NSES Science Content Standards
- Unifying concepts and processes in science
- Science as inquiry
- Life science

Find a rotting log on the school grounds or in a nearby wooded area. Have students predict what they think they will find when the log is gently turned over. A rotting log can be home to numerous arthropods, amphibians, fungi, and ferns. Students can expect to see sow bugs and pill bugs (terrestrial crustaceans), centipedes, millipedes, spiders, beetles, ants, termites, salamanders, snakes, and assorted other organisms. Several types of mosses, molds, and fungi will likely be growing in and on the log, along with other plants. Students can observe the various organisms they find by using resources such as field guides to identify the various organisms. They can also predict the functions of each item they observe, later doing research to determine why each item is there. If possible, students should observe the log several times over the course of the year, noting changes they see each time. This activity could even be continued for multiple years, passing down previous students' journals as a starting point for the next year's class. *Caution students to watch out for ticks, snakes, and harmful spiders.*

Activity 10. Comparing Flowers (preK–3)

NSES Science Content Standards

- Unifying concepts and processes in science
- Science as inquiry
- Life science

Colorful flowers generally catch the eye of young students and make a nice item to study in the schoolyard. In this activity, students locate a large flower and find at least five different structures on it. Then they compare the structures they found with a labeled drawing of a flower in a reference book. Challenge students to do the following:

- Compare different colors, shapes, smells, and structures of flowers.
- Choose at least five flowers of the same color and compare their shapes, smells, and structures.
- Compare five similar structures in at least three different kinds of flowers, and predict the function of each structure.
- Locate eight different flowers, each with a different number of petals, or eight flowers of the same color but with a different number of petals.
- Locate five flowers that have small green leaves (sepals) directly below the colored petals.

Activity 11. Comparing Features of Trees (4–8)

NSES Science Content Standards

- Unifying concepts and processes in science
- Science as inquiry
- Life science

Topic: Identifying Trees
Go to: *www.scilinks.org*
Code: SYS006

Students generally have seen many different trees but often do not stop to really look at the similarities and differences, and what makes each species unique. These activities highlight specific features students can look for to appreciate the variation found in trees.

a. Comparing features in different conifer trees: evergreens (4–8)

It is not uncommon for students to use the term *pine* for all evergreen trees; however, at least six different types of evergreen trees grow in North America. Several of these are generally found around schools. In this activity, student teams examine the different types of evergreen trees in the schoolyard, making a list of the type of leaf, cone, branch, and bark found on each. Challenge the teams to come up with three clear distinguishing characteristics of each type of evergreen tree.

b. Comparing features in different deciduous trees (4–8)

As with evergreen trees, deciduous trees vary greatly from species to species. In this activity, student teams visit different deciduous trees on the school grounds, noting different characteristics of each tree. Challenge students to come up with three clear distinguishing characteristics of each type of deciduous tree.

c. Comparing features in conifers and deciduous trees (4–8)

Most students realize that evergreen trees look very different from deciduous trees, yet they have a hard time answering when asked to describe the differences. In this activity, teams visit several different evergreen trees around the schoolyard and list their similarities; the students then visit several different deciduous trees around the school grounds and list their similarities. Challenge students to come up with five differences between the evergreen trees and the deciduous trees. They can then apply these variations to life cycles and adaptations that improve survival.

Activity 12. Determining the Age of a Tree (4–8)

NSES Science Content Standards

- Unifying concepts and processes in science
- Science as inquiry
- Life science
- Earth and space science

Most students are aware that the number of rings in a cross section shows the age of a tree. However, they may not have taken the time to observe the variations in color and texture that create the appearance of these rings.

a. Determining the age of a tree trunk (4–8)

Plants that live and grow for several years leave evidence of this growth in many ways. This is most apparent in a tree trunk's continuous increase in girth. Year after year during the growing season, the water-conducting vessels in the trunk slowly become clogged with minerals, so new ones must be continuously produced. During the early part of the growing season the vessels produced by the tree are larger in circumference than the vessels produced in the middle of the summer, and the vessels produced in the autumn are smaller in circumference than those produced in midsummer. During nongrowth periods, the tree produces no vessels. This pattern establishes a contrast between the late autumn vessels and the early spring vessels, which creates the illusion of a ring. Most students have noticed rings on a cut tree trunk but may not have questioned how they are formed. The rings are more apparent when the trunk is wet from a rain and are even clearer when food coloring is applied to the trunk. First, challenge student teams to determine the age of a tree stump in the schoolyard. Then challenge them to determine what happens in a

tree that grows in a tropical area with no differences among the seasons. Will these trees have rings? Why or why not? They can also research weather patterns and natural events that may have affected tree growth, such as droughts or fires, to see if the effects of these events can be seen in the tree rings.

b. Determining the age of a woody twig (4–8)

A tree's branches and twigs grow the same way as the trunk, but because of their smaller girth they are harder to count. One alternative is to examine the outside of a branch and find (in most trees) the terminal bud scale scar where the branch stopped growing the previous season. The terminal scar completely surrounds the twig and resembles one or more wide lines. Other scars, left from the stem of earlier leaves or branches, can usually be seen on the sides of a woody branch, and tiny dots inside the scars are the remains of the vascular tissue that entered the leaf or branch. Challenge students to determine the age of a young branch from at least five different trees. Did natural events affect the growth of one type of tree more than others? Students can research these events, along with growth patterns of tree species, to improve their understanding of ecosystem interactions.

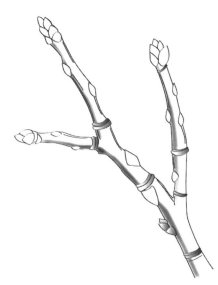

3 Creative Arts With Natural Materials

Activity 13. Making a Nature Treasure Chest (preK–3)
NSES Science Content Standards
- Life science
- Science and technology

Additional materials: bottle or jar, shoe box

This activity is great for students of all ages. To prepare, you must construct a map of a treasure chest full of nature items that are hinted at but not named. Roll the map into a cylinder and drop it into an old bottle or jar. A day or so before the class meets, bury the bottle or jar in the corner of the schoolyard. Create the treasure chest by placing several nature items (e.g., animal bones, types of seeds, evergreen cones, insect exoskeletons) in a shoe box and hiding it somewhere else in the yard. The day the class meets for this activity, student teams head into the field with the teacher and (somehow) discover the buried map. Students read the map and teams guess what the treasure chest contains. The remainder of the class time is spent searching for the treasure.

This activity can also be done as a scavenger hunt with notes hidden in various locations around the schoolyard that direct the teams to other locations with additional notes. Teams can be directed to a single treasure chest or to separate treasure chests holding different items.

Activity 14. Nature Photography (preK–8)
NSES Science Content Standards
- Science as inquiry
- Physical science
- Life science
- Earth and space science
- Science and technology
- Science in personal and social perspectives
- History and nature of science

Additional materials: disposable or digital cameras, or cell phones with cameras

Most students have their own digital camera and can capture images to download to a computer. This opportunity was not possible years ago, when the expenses of film and development were not included in a course budget. Photography opens up an incredibly exciting opportunity for students to create a pictorial record of their outdoor experiences. This record could be combined with a descriptive write-up for a field report, preparation of a pictorial presentation for the class, or creation of a virtual nature walk in which other teams can participate. One of our teams developed a storyboard about its experience in the outdoors.

Activity 15. Capturing Delicate Items in Nature With Spray Glue (preK–8)

NSES Science Content Standards
- Unifying concepts and processes in science
- Science as inquiry
- Life science
- Earth and space science
- Science in personal and social perspectives
- History and nature of science

Additional materials: spray glue, poster board or cardboard, kitchen tiles

Experienced students realize immediately that glue sprayed on a piece of cardboard captures everything it passes. Use this technique if you are interested in collecting delicate or fleeting items on school grounds. *Be aware of safety hazards associated with spray glue.*

- *Capturing seed dispersal from a dandelion:* Have students considered what the seeds of a dandelion scattered by a gust of wind look like the instant they are released? They can find out by spraying glue on a sheet of poster board and placing a carefully picked, seed-loaded dandelion head on the corner of the poster. As a teammate holds the board at face level, the experimenter should blow very hard at the side of the dandelion head, scattering the seeds onto the sticky card.
- *Capturing pollen released from a pine tree:* This is similar to the activity above, except a male pine cone is glued to the corner of a poster board instead of a dandelion head. When the blast of wind from the experimenter's mouth hits the side of the cone, tiny pollen grains are scattered outward onto the sticky mat.
- *Capturing the release of spores from a puffball mushroom:* Seeds and pollen are not the only items that can be trapped with spray glue. Spores released from a squeezed puffball can also be captured. A small puffball is placed on its side on the corner of the poster board, and the experimenter presses hard on the puffball with his or her thumb. This releases thousands of tiny spores from the puffball onto the sticky poster.
- *Capturing a spiderweb intact:* Spiderwebs are fascinating and beautiful, especially when they trap dew in the early morning. Because they are so intricate, spiderwebs are difficult to remove from their site in one piece for observation and study. An easy, accurate way for students to remove webs from a fixed site is to carefully have students walk through the web while holding a piece of poster board in front of them that has been coated liberally with spray glue. When this process is done correctly, the web will stick to the poster board exactly as it was positioned in the environment. Teams can try different colors of poster board for variation.

- *Capturing insect swarms in flight:* Almost everyone has experienced annoying gnats, bugs, and horseflies circling their heads, but rarely have they had a chance to see these insects with a magnifying glass. In this exercise, the experimenter can capture dozens of the insects on the sticky surface of a poster board and examine them closely with a magnifying lens. This exercise generally requires the assistance of a teammate. *Do not attempt to capture bees or other stinging insects!*

- *Capturing fur, feathers, footprints, and sometimes small animals:* Spray glue can be really sticky, capturing some unexpected items. An interesting activity is to spray glue on a wide board or kitchen tile and leave it overnight on the school grounds. Students can make predictions about what they will catch overnight with their sticky trap. These might include small mammals or insects. *Caution: Students should wear gloves and use caution when handling animals.*

- *Displaying ferns, leaves, twigs, and flowers on spray glue tiles:* Spray glue can be used in other ways besides capturing the above-mentioned organisms. If the projects that students perform are not going to be kept for a long period of time, participants can display their collection of nature items, such as leaves or ferns, easily and efficiently on tiles or posters sprayed with glue. It is important, however, that students allow the glue to dry thoroughly on the prepared surface, or else unwanted items will stick to the edges of the display.

Activity 16. Making Tracings of Plants (preK–3)

NSES Science Content Standards

- Unifying concepts and processes in science
- Science as inquiry
- Life science

Some items in the schoolyard that children can collect make wonderful tracings when placed on a flat surface and covered firmly with a clean sheet of unlined paper. Once the item and paper are correctly placed on a smooth surface, children can rub the covered item using the edge of a sharpened pencil or a colored crayon to reveal an exact replica of the item on the paper. Schoolyard objects such as leaves, soft-stemmed flowers, nonwoody stems, vines, ferns, and club mosses work well for tracing. Once they have finished, students compare shapes, vein patterns, and other properties of the items they have traced.

Tracings can also be done as the background; students make a natural design drawing on a thin piece of drawing paper by holding the paper against a surface that has definite texture, such as a smooth rock or the not-so-rough bark on a tree. They then rub a crayon completely over the paper, which transfers the texture to the paper. Some students transfer various textures to different sections of the paper or use different color crayons to add interest to their drawings.

Activity 17. Pressing Soft-Stemmed Plants (preK–8)

NSES Science Content Standards
- Unifying concepts and processes in science
- Science as inquiry
- Physical science
- Life science

Additional materials: cardboard, books, or other heavy objects to serve as weights

Many of the items collected in the activities described in this book will last much longer if the moisture in their cells is pressed out of the tissues. This can be done easily when nature items, such as flowers, are sandwiched between two sheets of thin cardboard and pressed under a pile of heavy books for 10–20 days. The pressing will work best if the environment in which the pressing is taking place has low humidity. What features are the same after items have been pressed and dried? What properties have changed?

Activity 18. Drying Plants (4–8)

NSES Science Content Standards
- Unifying concepts and processes in science
- Science as inquiry
- Life science

Drying items without pressing is a bit more difficult than pressing because students are removing the moisture from plants without squeezing it out. Many feel it is worth the effort, however, since the plants remain fuller and more robust. For this activity, students should pick the plants in the late morning after the dew has disappeared. They then select a cool, dry place indoors to hang their bundles of flowers or berries (no more than 8 or 10 plants per bundle). Students should hang their bundles of plants upside-down, which encourages them to dry. Experience shows that blue, orange, and pink flowers and berries will retain their colors best when dried. Students can compare features of the preserved plants with those of fresh plants to see how they have changed as moisture was removed from the tissues.

Activity 19. Making Plaster Molds of Animal Footprints (4–8)

NSES Science Content Standards
- Unifying concepts and processes in science
- Physical science
- Life science
- Science and technology

Additional materials: plaster, clay, clear acrylic spray or shellac, small box, bucket or container for mixing plaster

Students usually enjoy making plaster copies of impressions, particularly if the impression is an animal footprint left in sand or mud. If animal footprints cannot be located on the school grounds for this exercise, footprints can be designed with a clay that hardens and then pressed into the soft ground. Sticks, stones, or other obstructions must be cleaned out of the impression. Once the footprint is cleared, students slowly add water to the plaster in a small bucket or other container, stirring gently so a paste without lumps develops to the thickness of thick pancake syrup. This is best done at the site of the footprint since the mixture will start to harden immediately when the stirring stops. When the correct thickness is produced, students carefully pour the mixture into the impression so it covers the footprint entirely. Allow the plaster to harden and dry before removing it from the ground. Check the package to determine the approximate hardening time for the plaster you use. If the plaster mold is to be retained for a long period, shellac, varnish, or clear acrylic spray can be used to coat the dried cast. Plaster molds can also be made from impressions of hands, leaves, coins, and buttons. *Be sure to work in a well-ventilated area when using varnish, shellac, or spray acrylic.*

   Plaster can also be used to replicate the three-dimensional form of a plant or animal. When making a cast, students need a small natural item they have found in the schoolyard (e.g., snail shell or acorn) and a small paper or cardboard box containing damp soil that will hold its shape (some teachers may prefer to use a flattened piece of modeling clay in place of damp soil). Students press the three-dimensional item deep into the soil or clay, then carefully remove it so a clear impression of the item remains. The plaster is mixed thoroughly with water to the consistency of thick syrup, then poured into the impression. After the plaster has set, the box can be gently torn open and the soil or clay removed from around the replicated three-dimensional image. Other natural items that work well with this activity are dead bugs, hard fruits or seeds, and bones.

Activity 20. Recycling (4–8)
NSES Science Content Standards
- Unifying concepts and processes in science
- Life science
- Science and technology
- Science in personal and social perspectives
- History and nature of science

Additional materials: mixing containers (20a); eggbeaters or blenders (optional) (20a); screens (old window screens work well) (20a); large, flat pans (20a); rolling pins (20a); assorted materials for decorations (20a); assorted household or school waste items (20b)

There are numerous ways to teach students about recycling. Composting is one way and is discussed elsewhere in this book, but you may want to try some other projects. One simple way to create a usable end product from waste materials around the school is to make paper from scraps being thrown away. This activity can be messy, so choose an appropriate location on the school grounds.

SCI LINKS.
THE WORLD'S A CLICK AWAY

Topic: Recycling
Go to: *www.scilinks.org*
Code: SYS008

a. Make your own paper. (4–8)

Recycling paper is a simple project that produces a usable end product. Basic project materials include paper, water, and a mixing container of some kind, although eggbeaters or blenders can make the finished product smoother. Class members collect old paper, such as newspaper, construction paper, copier paper, tablet paper, wrapping paper, or other scraps from around the school. Students tear these papers into small pieces, place them in a container, and add enough water to cover the paper. Once the paper has soaked up as much water as possible (a few hours or overnight), students pour off the excess water. If the class has access to a blender, students pour the mixture into the blender and blend until smooth. If not, they can mix it thoroughly with their hands or use an eggbeater to blend the paper and water into pulp. Next, students place a screen over a large flat pan and pour the pulp onto the screen. The mixture needs to be spread out so it is as thin and as smooth as possible. Once this is done, students cover the pulp with waxed paper and use a smooth piece of wood or a rolling pin to squeeze out as much water as they can. Students carefully remove the waxed paper and let their paper dry for a day or two in a secure area of the school grounds. Several variations of the activity are possible once the basics have been mastered. Students can consider adding glitter, flowers, leaves, or seeds as decorations. They also may decide to use cookie and candy molds to make shapes instead of flat sheets of paper. Students can use their recycled paper to make the cover of a nature journal or storybook they have written.

b. Additional recycling ideas (4–8)

Students can do several other activities to recycle household and school waste. One fun idea is a recycled fashion show, where students make clothing or accessories from waste materials. Students can also find unusual uses for bottle caps, aluminum cans, egg cartons, plastic grocery bags, plastic containers of various shapes and sizes, string, yarn, and almost anything else in designing craft projects or posters to illustrate other science activities. Have an outdoor sculpture contest on the school grounds using cardboard boxes and other scraps, perhaps in conjunction with a recycled fashion show. Other classes can tour the artwork and judge the fashions to learn about recycling.

4 A Look at Lower Plants

NSES Science Content Standards

- Unifying concepts and processes in science
- Science as inquiry
- Life science

Additional materials: magnifying glasses (21a, b, c)

While many simple plants are microscopic, some freshwater types are colonial and mass together, making them large enough to see without a microscope. In this activity, students use magnifying glasses to observe the diversity of lower plant groups in the schoolyard.

Remind students not to view the Sun with the magnifying glasses.

a. Examining algae (4–8)

Algae are found in slow-moving or still bodies of water around the schoolyard. What makes this activity a bit tricky is the fact that the algae will likely be mixed in with other single-celled "bugs" in a pond scum called *infusoria*. Infusions like this develop quickly in

Topic: Plant
Characteristics
Go to: www.scilinks.org
Code: SYS009

freshwater that sits in the Sun for some time. Many teachers who have done this activity suggest putting a few fragments of lettuce, grass clippings, or a pinch of fertilizer in the water to encourage growth. In this activity, students use their magnifying glass to locate five different types of nonfilamentous algae in a drop of the infusion. Alternatively, students can find five different types of algae filaments. Finally, with their magnifying glasses, students can find five different types of nonfilamentous colonial algae.

b. Examining mosses (4–8)

Students are often surprised at how many different types of moss they can find on the school grounds. In a large, sunny yard, students can usually locate 8–10 different mosses, some of which have reproducing stalks and capsules rising from the tops of individual plants. Challenge teams in this activity to locate 5 different types of mosses, 5 different locations of mosses, 5 different types of mosses with filaments and capsules coming out their tops, 5 different types of mosses with filaments or capsules coming off their sides, and 5 different types of mosses without filaments or capsules on the school grounds.

c. Examining liverworts (4–8)

Most students have never seen liverworts, yet they can be found in places with a lot of moisture. If the schoolyard has a fast-moving stream that cascades over rocks, students could find liverworts. There are two major kinds of liverworts: the leathery, flattened body type called *thallus* and the leaflike or stringy type called *leafy*. See if the students can find both types on rocks in the stream or alongside the fast-moving water.

Activity 22. Observing Lichens (4–8)

NSES Science Content Standards

- Unifying concepts and processes in science
- Science as inquiry
- Life science

Additional materials: magnifying glasses

Lichens are a perfect example of symbiosis because each type is actually made up of an algae and a fungus that need each other for survival. There are three major kinds of lichens (*crustose, foliose,* and *fruticose*), and each holds an enormous variety of features. This variety opens up the potential for student teams to locate many of these characteristics. One challenge presented to teams might be to ask students to locate least five different types of lichens growing on different trees and compare their sizes, shapes, colors, and textures. Alternatively, students can compare five different types of lichens growing on a single tree and measure their sizes, shapes, colors, and textures. Another option is for students to locate as many different types of lichens growing on nontree surfaces as they can. Challenge advanced groups with questions such as whether different types of lichens prefer different types of trees or whether they are always found growing on the same side of the trees.

Activity 23. Observing Fungi (4–8)

NSES Science Content Standards

- Unifying concepts and processes in science
- Science as inquiry
- Life science

Topic: Fungi
Go to: *www.scilinks.org*
Code: SYS010

Students recognize that molds grow on objects that are dead or dying, but few realize that fungi and molds are constantly around them in their homes, shopping malls, and schoolyard. Many students do not realize the tremendous array of colors, anatomies, and growth patterns displayed by molds and fungi. One reason for mold's incredible abundance is the ability to use spores, which do not require fertilization to grow and develop. The activity of capturing spore prints from a mushroom cap is described below. Fungi take on a variety of forms in nature; some are slimy (slime mold), some are gelatinous (jelly fungus), some are "cobwebby" (bread mold), some are bowl-like (bladder cups), some look like fingers (coral fungus), and some are smelly (stinkhorns). In this activity, challenge students to locate five different types of fungi around the schoolyard. *Be sure to find out about any student allergies to mold before doing this activity.*

Activity 24. Observing Mushrooms (preK–8)

NSES Science Content Standards

- Unifying concepts and processes in science
- Science as inquiry
- Life science

Mushrooms are one of the most familiar types of fungi and can be found in surprising locations in and around a schoolyard. Once students have started to be more observant about items in the natural world, they will be able to spot many examples that previously would have gone unnoticed.

a. A closer look at mushrooms (4–8)

Most students think there are only two or three different kinds of mushrooms in their environment. As they become more observant through careful searching, students are always surprised at how many kinds they can find. This activity's objective is to have students locate five different types of mushrooms in the schoolyard. Alternatively, they can find three different cell surfaces under the cap of mushrooms, three different textures of mushroom caps, three different directions in which the mushroom stem grows out of the site it is attached to, or five mushrooms with stems of different lengths or thicknesses.

A word of caution: Students should never bite into a mushroom or put their fingers in their mouths while looking for mushrooms. They should also wash their hands after this activity.

b. Spore prints from mushroom caps (preK–8)

Most students have seen mushrooms, but many do not realize that the portion they see is just a small section the fungi's body—the bulk of the mushroom is under the ground or in the log where it is growing. The function of the visible mushroom structure is the dispersal of the reproductive cells. The tiny cells or spores are easily seen when the mushroom cap has been left resting, smooth side down, on a clean sheet of paper for several days. Students must keep the mushroom cap and paper dry over this time. After four or five days, student teams should remove the mushroom cap to reveal a circular pattern made up of thousands of spores. Different types of mushrooms leave different colors of spores, and when the spores are viewed under a magnifier they take on different shapes. Team members should record the colors, shapes, and spore patterns in their field reports. Although mushrooms are available in the spring and early summer, the best time for students to find mushrooms in the schoolyard is late summer and fall.

Activity 25. Growing Mushrooms (4–8)

NSES Science Content Standards
- Unifying concepts and processes in science
- Science as inquiry
- Life science

Additional materials: wood mulch or compost mix, hot water (no more than 90°F), wide-mouth glass jar

This really fun exercise is not as easy as it first seems. Surprisingly, mushrooms are rather fickle about where they will grow. Students first create the growth medium, which can be either a compost of leaves, coffee grounds, and vegetable matter or a wood mulch mixture of sawdust, wood chips, and wheat straw. Once students have decided which medium to use, mix the materials with very hot water for 2–3 min. to reduce the harmful bacteria levels in the mixture. The water should not be boiling, or it will also destroy the good bacteria that provide the nutrients mushrooms need. Team members should allow the hot medium to cool for 15–20 min., then place it in a thoroughly washed, wide-mouth, glass jar (a large pickle or mayonnaise jar works well). Students need to select a ripe mushroom (with the gills fully exposed) from the school grounds and break it up over or into the growing medium. Finally, they need to make sure the medium is moist; loosely cover the jar; place it in a dark, warm area; and wait. Teams should check the jar periodically to ensure it remains moist but not wet.

Activity 26. Observing Shelf or Bracket Fungi (preK–8)

NSES Science Content Standards
- Unifying concepts and processes in science
- Science as inquiry
- Life science
- Science in personal and social perspectives

Mushroomlike growths frequently can be found sprouting like shelves from the trunks of trees. Sometimes these brackets are quite hard and other times they are quite soft, but no matter what texture they have, their function is always the same: to release reproductive cells to start another generation. In this exercise, student teams try to locate five different types of shelf fungi on trees in the schoolyard. Alternatively, students may try to locate five shelf fungi with different types of stems that hold them to the tree, three different cell surfaces under the cap of the shelf fungi, three different colors of shelf fungi, or three different textures (hard, medium, and soft) of shelf fungi surfaces.

The underside of some shelf fungi is very smooth and has a light color, making it an ideal surface for writing a stick message. Historians tell us that early humans drew figures on the underside of shelf fungi, and North American woodland Indians were known to leave messages for late-arriving travelers on the fungi as well. This is a fun activity, but students should not be permitted to destroy more than one or two brackets for messages.

This activity can also be done with birch bark, aspen bark, or beech bark and with "secret signs" such as stone piles, twig crosses, vine knots, and messages in mud or sand. *Note:* Students should never make marks in the bark of living trees, as this can damage or kill the tree.

Activity 27. Observing Ferns (4–8)

NSES Science Content Standards

- Unifying concepts and processes in science
- Science as inquiry
- Life science

Topic: Ferns
Go to: *www.scilinks.org*
Code: SYS011

As with many other lower plants, the numbers and types of ferns growing on the school grounds is surprising, especially if the area supports a number of different habitats. Before this activity, if students are asked how many different types of ferns they expect to find, they will probably say that two or three is the most that they expect to see. Challenge teams to locate five different types of ferns around the school. Add to the challenge by having them look for five different types of ferns with smooth edges, five different types of ferns with rough edges, five different types of ferns with dots (soria that will contain spores for reproduction) on their underside, five different types of ferns with their soria only along their edges, and five different types of ferns with the soria held high on a filament.

Young ferns of many species—known as fiddleheads because of their similarity to the coiled top of a violin—can be spotted in early spring emerging from the ground. Many people consider these a delicacy and gather them for consumption. Students on an early spring nature hike around the school can be challenged to spot these young ferns and can then watch their growth over the first few weeks of warmer weather. Have students measure the growth and plot it on graphs to see which type of fern grows fastest.

Other species of ferns can be seen all year. Old growth of these evergreen ferns can be seen all winter, only turning brown and drying up when the new spring growth starts. Find an area of the schoolyard where these are located and have students follow their growth cycle starting in the fall and continuing until the end of school. Ask students to describe the changes they see or to note when various parts of the plant appear, using their nature journals to record their observations.

5 More Complex Plants

Activity 28. A Close Look at Diversity in Higher Plants (4–8)

NSES Science Content Standards

- Unifying concepts and processes in science
- Science as inquiry
- Life science

It is fun not only to look around the schoolyard for the variety of living things but also to compare items that are similar. Features of many natural items can be compared or contrasted. Challenge students to do the following:

Topic: Plant Kingdom
Go to: *www.scilinks.org*
Code: SYS012

- Locate five features on twigs that serve the same function (e.g., buds) or five features on one branch that are different from the others (e.g., lenticels).
- Locate five leaves from different trees and compare them for shape, size, color, margin, texture, vein pattern, and length of stem. This comparison can also be done with five leaves from the same tree.
- Locate five different types of bark on different trees or shrubs growing in the schoolyard. Alternatively, have students find five different types of bark growing on a single mature tree. Students can also be challenged to find five different invertebrates living on or in the bark of standing trees.
- Locate at least 10 trees of different types, shapes, and heights in the schoolyard and think of ways to estimate their heights. Students can also be asked to sketch the variations they observe in their journals.
- Locate and compare at least five different structures bearing seeds on various deciduous and evergreen trees in the schoolyard. For example, have students compare the length of 25 cones from the same type of tree and calculate the average, or they can compare the internal structures of various types of cones. Students could also compare the internal structures of two different families of trees (e.g., pines and spruce). Students could be asked to locate at least five different structures bearing seeds on various shrubs, or to describe at least five different methods for trees or shrubs to disperse seeds.
- Locate five branches with buds coming off by themselves. Alternatively, locate five branches with buds coming off in pairs or five branches with buds coming off in groups of threes.
- Locate 5 plants with flowers of 2, 3, or 4 different colors. Alternatively, find 10 different shapes of petals on flowers.
- Locate five plants with different types of soft fruits around the schoolyard; locate five plants with different colors of soft fruits, or five fruits with different surfaces (smooth, bumpy). Students may also try to locate five plants with different types of hard fruits, five different plants with hard cases around fruits but with definite seams for splitting open, or five different plants with hard cases around fruits but without definite seams.

Remind students not to eat fruits they find, as some may be toxic.

Activity 29. Comparing Features of Monocots and Dicots (4–8)

NSES Science Content Standards

- Unifying concepts and processes in science
- Science as inquiry
- Life science

Topic: Parts of a Plant
Go to: *www.scilinks.org*
Code: SYS013

Additional materials: magnifying glass (29a, b), food coloring (29b)

Complex flowering plants can be divided into two major groups—monocots and dicots. These activities give students the opportunity to compare the features of these groups. *Remind students not to look at the Sun with magnifying glasses.*

a. Differences between monocots and dicots (4–8)

It is interesting that common soft-stemmed flowering plants can represent two very different groups, monocots and dicots. The terms come from the number of food reserves (called cotyledons) in the seed. Dicotyledons have two food reserves or seed leaves within the seed covering, while monocotyledons have just one. But students do not have to cut open a seed to determine if the plant they are investigating is a monocot or a dicot. Several visible features distinguish the two groups. Challenge students to find at least five distinguishing characteristics of soft-stemmed monocots and soft-stemmed dicots by using a magnifying glass to look at leaves, stems, and flowers of various plants.

- *Flower parts:* Monocots have flower parts in groups of 3, or multiples of 3 such as 6 or 9 (3 petals, 3 sepals, 3 stamens [male pollen producers] or 3 pistils [female egg producers]). Dicots have flower parts in groups of 4 or 5, or multiples of 4 or 5 such as 8 or 10 (4/5 petals, 4/5 sepals, 4/5 stamens, 4/5 pistils).
- *Vein patterns in the leaf:* Monocots have the veins running through their leaves in a parallel fashion. Dicots have the veins in their leaves running like fingers off a hand or the barbs coming off a shaft like a bird feather.
- *Vein pattern in the stem:* Monocots have veins running parallel within the stem. Dicots never have parallel veins in the stem.
- *Rooting system:* Monocots generally have a fibrous rooting system. Dicots generally have a taproot system.
- *Primary and secondary growth:* Monocots generally do not have secondary growth; dicots usually do have secondary growth.

b. Observing structures in a cross section of soft-stemmed monocots and dicots (4–8)

Soft-stemmed monocot and dicot plants have very different tissue arrangements inside their stems. To see this, students must cut cleanly across a large stem of each type and look at the cut surface in cross section under a magnifying glass. If time permits, the teams can place cut stems in a jar of red or blue food coloring for a few hours to delineate the differences. Challenge teams to find three differences between monocot stems and dicot stems.

Activity 30. Comparing the Anatomy of a Dicot Root With a Dicot Stem (4–8)

NSES Science Content Standards
- Unifying concepts and processes in science
- Science as inquiry
- Life science

Additional materials: magnifying glass, food coloring

Students can also compare the cross section of a root and a stem from a dicot plant. To do this, teams find a soft-stemmed dicot with a taproot and clean off the dirt and debris around the stem and root. Next, the students cut the stem and root cleanly across the diameter and place them in food coloring. After a few hours, students clean off the colored solution and use a magnifying glass to compare the cross-sectional cuts of the stem and the root. Challenge teams to find three differences between the two structures. *Remind students not to look at the Sun with magnifying glasses.*

Activity 31. Comparing a Soft-Stemmed Dicot With a Hard-Stemmed Dicot (4–8)

NSES Science Content Standards
- Unifying concepts and processes in science
- Science as inquiry
- Life science

Additional materials: magnifying glass, food coloring

In an activity similar to the previous one, students compare a soft-stemmed dicot with a hard-stemmed or woody dicot. In this activity, teams cut a stem off a woody branch that is about the same diameter as the soft-stemmed dicot and compare the two cross sections under magnification. To help delineate the two, teams can soak the ends of the stems in food coloring for a few hours before making the observation. Challenge teams to find three differences between the soft stem and the hard stem. *Remind students not to look at the Sun with magnifying glasses.*

Activity 32. Comparing the Leaves on Soft-Stemmed Plants (4–8)

NSES Science Content Standards

- Unifying concepts and processes in science
- Science as inquiry
- Life science

Students are often surprised to find that leaves are arranged differently on stems. With close examination, students can perform the following comparisons. In the schoolyard, challenge the students to locate

- five different plants with leaves that are arranged opposite each other;
- five different plants with leaves that are arranged in an alternate pattern; and
- five different plants with leaves that are arranged in whorls of three, four, or five.

Then increase the challenge by asking teams to find

- five different leaves with a small stem attached;
- five different leaves with no stem attached to the leaf blade;
- five different plants with very small, leaflike appendages at the junction of the main stem and smaller leaf stem;
- five leaves that are arranged along the side and at the end of the stem;
- five plants with a leaf that grows from the stem at a 45-degree angle; or
- five plants with two or more leaves growing from the same location.

Activity 33. Dissecting Flowers (4–8)

NSES Science Content Standards

- Unifying concepts and processes in science
- Science as inquiry
- Life science

Additional materials: tweezers or forceps

Like animal structures, plant structures are complex, with numerous different parts. By dissecting a flower and observing how the parts fit together, students can see how form and function create the final product. It is important that students take their time in removing and identifying the various structures of a flower. Using tweezers or forceps, student teams should remove each structure from a flower and place each separately on a sheet of paper. See if teams can isolate 10 different structures. While some team members are removing the anatomical parts, others can begin determining the function of the structures being isolated. When the items have all been removed, displayed, and given a function, team members can create a name for each structure before looking up the proper scientific term in a reference book.

Activity 34. Sprouting Seeds (preK–8)

NSES Science Content Standards

- Unifying concepts and processes in science
- Science as inquiry
- Life science

Additional materials: covered shirt box, waxed paper

Topic: Seed
Germination
Go to: *www.scilinks.org*
Code: SYS014

Student teams can find dozens of seeds around the schoolyard. Some seeds come from mature plants around the school, and other seeds have been transported by various means. Teams of students should carefully check the area around the school to find five different kinds of seeds. To initiate sprouting in the seeds, students must soak them in a container of water for several hours. Then they remove the seeds and place them between two layers of moist paper towels in a covered shirt box lined with waxed paper. Students place the box on a dark shelf in a site protected from the weather. After a few days, they examine the box for germinating seeds. If the seeds have just begun to sprout, students can lightly remoisten the paper towels and return the box to the protected shelf. Once the seeds germinate enough to have both the root and shoot showing, teams should try to determine which is which.

Activity 35. Studying Plant Tropism (4–8)

NSES Science Content Standards

- Unifying concepts and processes in science
- Science as inquiry
- Physical science
- Life science

Topic: Plant Tropism
Go to: *www.scilinks.org*
Code: SYS015

Additional materials: jars or other containers

Students can study both positive and negative geotropism using the seeds that sprouted in the previous activity. To check whether they correctly distinguished the stem end from the root end, students can roll several dry paper towels into a cylinder and secure the roll loosely with a rubber band. They should carefully place several germinating seeds of the same species between layers of paper towels in different directions (upright, sideways, and upside-down) and place the cylinder vertically in a jar containing an inch of water (so the bottom of the cylinder is in the water). Making sure the seeds do not shift, students then place the jar in a dark, protected area for several days. After that time, teams should remove the cylinder from the jar and carefully unroll the paper towels. They should record what they have found in their field reports and try to determine why the germinating seeds look different from each other.

Activity 36. Seed Dispersal Techniques (preK–8)

NSES Science Content Standards

- Unifying concepts and processes in science
- Science as inquiry
- Physical science
- Life science

Plants have developed an amazing repertoire of creative seed dispersal techniques. Students are often unaware, for example, that common items such as the maple "helicopters" are actually seeds, specially adapted for wind dispersal. In addition, seeds can be dispersed by sticking to animals, floating in water, and being eaten, as well as through unique mechanisms such as mini-explosions. First, ask students to identify different kinds of seeds and then challenge them to discover 10 ways in which seeds are spread to new areas. Once they have come up with several ideas, students can find seeds in various habitats around the school. While many may be familiar with common flower and vegetable seeds, encourage them to think about trees, grass, burdock, and other plants they may see. Students can then collect different types of seeds and compare how they work to move the seed to a new location. Dandelions, fruit (apples, pears, and berries), helicopter seeds from maples or ashes, acorns from oak trees, sunflowers, and pinecones are all good examples. Students should think about how the seeds from a raspberry bush or other local shrubs are moved to a new place. The teacher may need to introduce the idea of using an animal's digestive tract to help with dispersal. Students can look at the features of plants whose seeds are dispersed by wind. Challenge students to find at least 8 examples of wind-dispersed seeds, and ask them to find other ways animals help with seed dispersal. This can lead to examples such as burdock and other seeds that cling to fur and clothing.

Once students have had a chance to examine and compare different seeds, challenge them to design their own giant seed. They can determine how it will be transported and then build it using classroom materials such as paper, string, paper clips, and other craft supplies. Encourage students to take the seeds outside to test them.

Activity 37. Locating the Numbers and Kinds of Seedlings in a Field: Succession (4–8)

NSES Science Content Standards

- Unifying concepts and processes in science
- Science as inquiry
- Life science
- Earth and space science
- Science in personal and social perspectives

Additional materials: field guides and identification resources

Many students do not realize that old fields hold miniature forests made up of a variety of trees. The trees are difficult to spot in the winter, but when they sprout with their characteristic leaves in the spring, they are easily identified. If students watch the site throughout the spring, summer, and autumn, they will notice some saplings are doing better than others. This competition to dominate the area is called succession. With this information, teams can predict the eventual dominant tree species in the evolving forest, along with the kinds of animals that arrive to reside in these developing habitats. This can be an excellent ongoing project, with each class doing a survey that is saved. Each year, students can compare their results to those from previous years, noting which plants have survived and grown and which ones were not able to compete as the habitat changed.

Activity 38. Studying Transpiration in Plants (4–8)

NSES Science Content Standards

- Unifying concepts and processes in science
- Science as inquiry
- Life science
- Earth and space science

Additional materials: potted plants, dishes for water, plastic bags, string

Topic: How Do Plants Respond to Their Environment?
Go to: www.scilinks.org
Code: SYS016

Students are usually surprised to learn that water moves through a plant constantly unless the soil is exceedingly dry. This process can be demonstrated in numerous ways. One easy method is to get a plant in a flower pot, put it in a small container of water, and place this in a small plastic shopping bag. Have the students mark the top level of the water in the container, raise the sides of the bag, and use a string to secure the neck of the bag around the top of the flower pot, leaving the plant above the closed neck of the bag. The students should let the plant sit for several hours. As the flower pot rests in the water, ask students to record in their field reports the environmental conditions of the location (e.g., sunny, warm, and still air from 10:00 a.m. to 2:00 p.m.). Students should also record the surrounding temperature each hour (10:00 a.m., 11:00 a.m., noon, 1:00 p.m., and 2:00 p.m.). At the end of the day, students loosen the bag and, using a ruler to measure, record the amount of water that has disappeared from the container. This is the amount of water that has moved through the plant in four hours on that particular day. The experiment should be repeated on a (1) warm, cloudy day; (2) warm, rainy day; (3) warm, windy day; and (4) warm, windy, and rainy day during the same time span, again noting the hourly fluctuation of the temperature and variations in other weather conditions. This experiment can be done during different seasons to note the variation as the plant grows throughout the year.

Activity 39. Studying the Flow of Water in Soft-Stemmed Plants (4–8)

NSES Science Content Standards
- Unifying concepts and processes in science
- Science as inquiry
- Life science

Additional materials: containers for water, food coloring, plastic shopping bag, string

When the previous activity is performed, students may question whether the water is actually moving through the stem of the plant. A fun way to show that water does indeed move through the stem is to place several freshly cut soft-stemmed plants in a container of water that has a fairly dark color (add several drops of food coloring [not green] to the water). Have students pull a plastic shopping bag up around the rim of the container and loosely tie string around the stems. Leave the plants in a protected, sunny location for at least five hours. When the class returns later that day, they will see that the food coloring has moved up the stem and colored the leaves and flowers on the soft-stemmed plant. After the darkened tops are observed, students can cut through the soft tissue and see the darkened xylem vessels in the stem cross section.

This activity can be performed by different teams as each group collects its own bunch of soft-stemmed plants and performs the experiment separately. Students like seeing who ends up with the darkest leaves. Students can also cut the stem in half vertically, starting at the bottom and stopping a third of the way up to the top of the plant. After cutting, place one half of the stem in one color of water and the other half in a different color of water. Note the two different color tops. This can also be done with different monocots (parallel-veined leaves) and dicots (nonparallel leaves) plants.

Activity 40. Comparing Structures of Aquatic Plants and Land Plants (4–8)

NSES Science Content Standards

- Unifying concepts and processes in science
- Science as inquiry
- Life science

Topic: Aquatic Plants and Animals
Go to: *www.scilinks.org*
Code: SYS017

Additional materials: magnifying glasses

Generally speaking, complex plants can be found in two different habitats on Earth, in water and on land. Students find it interesting that despite the differences between the habitats, there are as many similarities as there are differences between aquatic plants and land plants. In this activity, teams visit sites on and around the school grounds to compare the anatomical and functional differences between the plants. Challenge the teams to come up with five major similarities and five major differences between aquatic and terrestrial plants. *Remind students not to look at the Sun with magnifying glasses.*

> Aquatic plants always possess long underground stems from which leaves arise; each leaf tends to be large and rounded and floats on the water's surface. In addition, because the leaves of aquatic plants rest on the water surface, they have their *stomata* (air exchange pores) on the top surface of the leaf.

Activity 41. A Close Look at Roots (4–8)

NSES Science Content Standards

- Unifying concepts and processes in science
- Science as inquiry
- Life science

Unless a tree topples over in the immediate area, students rarely see the parts of a plant that are underground. While they are certainly aware of roots, few students have taken the time to examine them closely.

a. Comparing external structures on roots (4–8)

Most students know that *root* is the name given to many of a plant's underground structures. Older students may also be familiar with the different types of roots, including *taproots, fibrous roots, rhizobia* (leguminous roots), *prop roots, aerial roots,* and the various structures that come off the main root (*secondary roots* and *root hairs*). Unfortunately, students often memorize the terminology without witnessing the structures themselves. This is particularly disappointing with plant roots, which are not difficult to find. If students are challenged to find examples of the different structures of roots, they will be successful most of the time.

Topic: Roots
Go to: *www.scilinks.org*
Code: SYS018

Provide each team with a large spoon or trowel and ask teams to find an example of each structure. Remind them, however, that they must not leave any evidence that they have removed a part of the plant (such as a hole in the ground).

b. Discovering things that are and are not plant roots (4–8)

Once students understand the structural components of roots, they will be able to differentiate between roots and other plant structures that are found underground. After reviewing the structural anatomy of a root, challenge students to find at least three underground plant structures around the schoolyard that have the correct anatomy to be called a root and three underground plant structures that do not fit this category.

Underground plant structures that are roots:
taproot (radish, dandelion, evening primrose, goatsbeard, chicory), fibrous roots (reed grass, daylily), and rhizobia-leguminous roots (peas, soybean)

Underground plant structures that are not roots:
rhizomes (violets, ginger, irises, cattails), tubers (ground nut, bugleweed, spring beauty, orphine), bulbs (onion, garlic, leeks, calla lily, daffodils), stolons (strawberry), corms (gladiola), suckers (raspberry, blackberry)

6 Schoolyard Gardens and Nature Areas

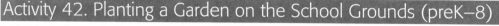

Activity 42. Planting a Garden on the School Grounds (preK–8)

NSES Science Content Standards

- Unifying concepts and processes in science
- Science as inquiry
- Life science
- Earth and space science
- Science in personal and social perspectives
- History and nature of science

Additional materials: flower and vegetable seeds (42a,b,c); topsoil, compost (see Activity 43), and/or fertilizer if needed (42a,b,c,d); garden tools (42a,b,c,d); greenhouse materials as needed (42c); milk jugs or cans (42d)

Topic: Plant Growth
Go to: *www.scilinks.org*
Code: SYS019

Gardens are not new to most students, but few have had the experience of working in one. Once involved, students ask a variety of questions, most of which are interesting and insightful. Some questions may lead to valid independent study projects. Planning a garden is fun and students should be actively involved in the decision making. To direct their ideas, encourage students to walk around schools, churches, homes, and parks in the vicinity of the school. As they walk, suggest they consider natural elements—such as sunlight, wind, and water relationships—and human factors—such as playgrounds, sidewalks, and parking lots—and particularly the way these factors would interact on the school grounds. With these factors in mind, work with the class to plan the garden during the late winter. Make sure you also check with administrators and school grounds personnel to identify sites that should be left undisturbed so plants are not mowed or destroyed inadvertently.

Once the garden is planned, the students can begin to grow plants indoors or in a makeshift greenhouse, such as those described in 42c. Following planting instructions at this point is crucial, since seedlings and shoots will reach their transplant periods at different times. Also, check with local nurseries to see if they would like to donate young plants.

As the weather warms, students should prepare the garden space for planting on the school grounds, as it will need to be turned and weeded. Good quality topsoil and a bit of fertilizer or compost (if needed) should be mixed with the soil. This phase takes time and may require students to work after school or spend some weekend hours on the project. Parents and family members often volunteer with this preparation, and students benefit greatly from this intergenerational experience. Students also enjoy planting and maintaining the garden. Guide the students as they select where specific plants will be placed. Consider subdividing the garden into zones so that each team has its own small garden patch to maintain. *Use caution when handling and applying chemicals such as fertilizers.*

a. Set an example—plan an environmentally friendly garden (4–8)

Encourage students to consider using environmentally friendly substitutes for pesticides, fungicides, and chemical fertilizers. To prepare the garden's soil, students should spread 2 or 3 in. of compost (see Activity 43) over the ground and mix it into the soil. Students should spread mulch, such as shredded leaves or bark, between the rows of plants to protect the soil and suppress weed growth. To prevent fungi from harming the plants, students can spray plants with a "home brew" mixture of water (1 gal.), baking soda (3 tbsp.), and canola oil or Murphy's Oil Soap (1 tbsp.). The baking soda reduces the acidic pH, which mildews and fungi love, and the oil soap helps the fluid stick to the plant. Students should spray the plants once a week in the cool of the morning. For insect pests, students can mix 1 tbsp. of ground red pepper with ½ gal. water, along with a few drops of dishwashing soap to discourage insects. Garlic works too (1 part 99% garlic concentrate, 1 part fish oil, and 98 parts water). For ease of measuring, use a 1 L bottle or container and add 10 ml each of the garlic concentrate and fish oil, then fill with water. Creating this dilution also is an excellent way to incorporate math skills into a science activity. Students should spray either concoction on the plants about once a week. They should also consider using biological insecticides such as Bt (Bacillus thuringiensis) to snuff out insect larva such as hornworms and cabbageworms. Students can use plants that encourage beneficial insects and discourage the not-so-beneficial pests. Helpful insects such as aphid midges, ladybugs, lacewings, dragonflies, ichneumon wasps, braconid wasps, and tachinid flies can be attracted to the garden by adding shallow water baths and cultivating pollen-rich plants such as alyssum, dill, cosmos, and yarrow.

b. Select easy-to-grow, colorful plants (preK–8)

For a successful garden, students might want to plant easy-to-grow perennials and bulbs. Below is a list of dependable perennials likely to lead to a garden full of healthy plants.

- April—daffodils (*Hypoxis* spp.), columbines (*Aquitegia* spp.), bleeding hearts (*Dicentra eximia*)
- May—peonies (*Paeonia* spp.), violets (*Viola* spp.), daisies (*Chrysanthemun* spp.), geraniums (*Geranium* spp.)
- June—coreopsis (*Coreopsis* spp.), iris (*Iris* spp.), black-eyed Susans (*Rudbeckia* spp.)
- July—daylilies (*Hemerocallis* spp.), Virginia bluebells (*Mertensia virginica*)
- August—obedient plants (*Physistegua* spp.), cardinal flowers (*Lorlia* spp.), steeple bushes (*Spiraea* spp.)
- September—asters (*Aster* spp.), hibiscus (*Hibiscus* spp.), phlox (*Phlox* spp.)

It is also fun to grow vegetables in a garden, and if they are selected carefully, they can be grown and eaten in their young state (before they mature) before summer vacation. Lettuce is a vegetable that can be raised and picked in a little more than a month. Other vegetables that can be grown in six to eight weeks are beans, beets, carrots, eggplant, and squash. Pumpkins are fun to plant and watch grow over the summer as well, and they take minimum gardening effort. When students return to the schoolyard at the end of the summer, they will be greeted with long, twisted vines that can be herded into a small area. Students love to watch the fruits grow during the fall, and they can harvest several pumpkins before Halloween.

c. Creating a mini-greenhouse (preK–8)

Several different types of greenhouses are easy and inexpensive to make for use around a school. All greenhouses follow the same principles in that they allow sunlight and small amounts of air and moisture to get to the plants while retaining the heat from solar energy. This allows students to start seeds early and transplant them when spring arrives.

- *The cloche greenhouse.* This is one of the simplest schoolyard greenhouses to make. Students use scissors or a knife to cut the neck off a clear, 2 L plastic bottle, and turn the bottle upside-down over small plants. Once this is done, students punch a few pencil-size holes around the middle of the bottle to allow ventilation and stop fungal diseases. *With younger students, the teacher should cut the bottle.*
- *The porch greenhouse.* Another simple greenhouse students can make involves lining a middle-size cardboard box (e.g., office paper box) with a plastic bag and putting 2 or 3 in. of garden soil on the plastic. Teams should select the seeds they wish to grow and follow seed package directions to plant them. Students add enough water to get the soil really damp, cover the top of the box with clear plastic wrap, and use duct tape to tape it to the sides of the box. Poke a few holes in the plastic wrap at the top so the seeds can get air, and place the box in a sunny spot outdoors. Be sure to protect the greenhouse from torrential downpours and icy temperatures by making sure it is in a protected location or by bringing it inside temporarily.
- *The plastic sheet greenhouse.* Students can plant the seeds they wish to grow directly in the garden in early spring, but they must protect the young seeds and

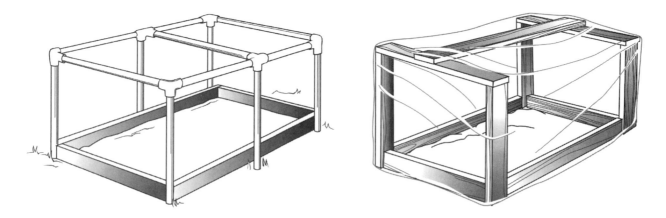

shoots from frost while retaining the Sun's heat. The easiest way to do this is to create a greenhouse with a sheet of transparent plastic that is held a few inches off the ground by a frame made of wood or plastic pipe. The plastic should be taped or tacked firmly to the frame so that it does not sag onto the growing plants; the plastic should also completely cover the ends and sides of the frame.

d. Transplanting plants from one place to another (4–8)

Transplanting foliage can be tricky. Sometimes it is wise to follow gardening suggestions from our ancestors. They recommended transplanting plants when the soil is wet. This way, the water creates a tighter fit between the soil and the roots, preventing air pockets from forming and harming the plants. Our ancestors recommended transplanting vegetation on cloudy or drizzly days or in the early morning or evening, when the sun is not as strong. Once they have moved the plants, students should protect the new transplants from heat, cold, or wind by placing a topless plastic milk jug or soft fabric over the plants to protect them from bad weather. Our ancestors also knew to transplant vegetables deeply (not shallowly) and, if the rooting systems of the plants were intertwined or fragile, to transplant them using cloth wraps or peat pots. They also recommended wrapping shiny metal, such as aluminum foil, loosely around the stems to repel insect pests. Some experienced gardeners suggest using a can opener to take both ends off empty cat food or tuna cans, then surrounding the young shoots with the round cylinder. This prevents harmful larva such as cutworms from destroying the young plants. Students can also consult experienced relatives and adult friends who might have suggestions.

Activity 43. Composting (preK–8)
NSES Science Content Standards
- Unifying concepts and processes in science
- Science as inquiry
- Life science
- Science in personal and social perspectives
- History and nature of science

Additional materials: containers, organic materials, worms, sticks or spoons for stirring the compost

Creating classroom compost can be done very easily around the school grounds, allowing students to turn ordinary waste into high-quality soil. There are different types, including lunchroom or kitchen compost and yard or garden compost. Have students determine which type they want to make, or have groups make different kinds and compare the results. They can also predict what will happen if they alter other variables, such as the size of the items being composted (leave them in large pieces or cut them up), the addition of water, or the location of the compost container (sun or shade). Place the organic materials to be composted in a container in a secure area of the school grounds.

Topic: Composting
Go to: *www.scilinks.org*
Code: SYS020

Clear plastic containers allow students to see what is happening, but wooden boxes, wire mesh enclosures, or most other containers also work well. Be sure the container has a lid to keep animals out of the compost. Once the organic materials are in the composter, add a layer of soil to cover them. Worms are also beneficial, so try to get dirt that has worms in it, or buy some worms at a bait store. Alternate layers if there is enough material, or add to the compost by placing more layers on top every few days. Once the compost gets warm, it needs to be turned or stirred. This is a good project for different teams. If students stir the compost every few days, the compost will become dark and crumbly. Compost should also be kept moist (not wet), and it will require air. Students should make sure there are spaces for air circulation. Once the compost is ready, students can then plant seeds in plain soil and soil mixed with compost and compare the results.

Activity 44. Making a Scarecrow to Chase Pests From the Garden (preK–8)

NSES Science Content Standards

* Science in personal and social perspectives

Additional materials: old clothes; straw or newspaper; waterproof paint or markers; coat hangers or wire; pillowcase; safety pins; string, rope, or tape

Students of all ages love to make scarecrows, especially if each team of students can create their own version. Students are always willing to contribute materials to create their scarecrow, donating old pants, shirts, gloves, socks, and accessories to the project. To make the scarecrow, students tie the ends of the legs on a pair of pants and the ends of the sleeves of a shirt using string, rope, or tape and stuff them with newspaper or other stuffing. Students should also stuff gloves and socks and fasten them with safety pins to the ends of the arms and legs. A pillowcase makes a great head and it easily pins to the neck of the shirt when ready. Before the students add the stuffing to the head, they should lightly pencil a face onto the pillowcase; using a pencil allows students to easily make adjustments if needed. When all students agree on the facial features, they finish the face with waterproof markers or paint. After the face dries, students can secure a hat to the pillowcase with safety pins and add other accessories. Some students have the scarecrow sit on a chair or bench, but most teams attach the scarecrow in a standing position to a metal or wooden stake for the spring, summer, and autumn. Arms and legs can be held out using a coat hanger or stout wire run through the sleeves or up a pant leg. Do not leave the scarecrow out in the winter, especially since there are not crops for the scarecrow to protect during that season.

Activity 45. Counting Dominant and Recessive Traits in a Vegetable Garden (4–8)

NSES Science Content Standards

- Unifying concepts and processes in science
- Science as inquiry
- Life science

SC*LINKS*
THE WORLD'S A CLICK AWAY

Topic: Plant
Characteristics
Go to: *www.scilinks.org*
Code: SYS009

Vegetables such as corn and beans were among the earliest plants studied. The mono and dihybrid genetics of the plants were described by Gregor Mendel in the late 19th century. For dominance to be observed, however, students must wait for the sprouts to grow into older plants. After the plants are fully grown, team members walk among the rows of plants and record in their field reports inherited characteristics such as height, shape, and the seed or fruit color in the maturing plants. Students should keep records of the observations in their field report, and ratios of the characteristics should be calculated for the plants. This can be done with either cultivated or wild types of plants.

Activity 46. Investigating Self-Pollination and Cross-Pollination in Plants (4–8)

NSES Science Content Standards

- Unifying concepts and processes in science
- Science as inquiry
- Life science
- Science in personal and social perspectives

Additional materials: plastic bags, forceps or tweezers

Complex monocots and dicots require pollen to travel from male reproductive structures (stamens) to female reproductive structures (pistils) in flowers, so it is easy to intercept the pollen and divert it to flowers that generally are not destined to receive it. Nature discourages some plants from self-fertilizing by growing the female receptors much higher in the air and keeping the pollen producers in the lower parts of the flower to discourage self-pollination (spatial disruption), or creating a lag period between the time pollen is released by the male organs and the receptive time for fertilization in the female organs (temporal disruption). Sometimes flower parts form barriers to separate the union of sex cells from the same plant.

- *Finding flowers with different ways of discouraging self-pollination.* In this challenge, students try to find three flowers with structures that discourage pollen transfer to the same plant.

- *Finding flowers with ways of encouraging self-pollination.* Similar to the last experiment, students try to find three flowers with structures that encourage pollen transfer to the same plant.
- *Finding flowers that produce only male-reproducing cells or only female-reproducing cells.* In this exercise, teams should try to find three different plants that have just one type of reproductive organ, focusing on species with separate male and female plants.
- *Manually intercepting pollen from one flower and transferring it to another.* In this activity, teams come up with a way to get pollen from one plant to another manually. If the team can come up with a valid procedure, they should establish their system of manual fertilization with several plants in the schoolyard.

Topic: Plant
    Reproduction
Go to: *www.scilinks.org*
Code: SYS021

This activity requires students to encase in plastic lunch bags flowers of a single species that normally do not cross-pollinate. One student should pull female receptors (pistils) off the flowers with forceps at the time the plant normally releases its pollen. A student then ties the neck of the bags to prevent pollen from escaping. At the same time, a teammate should pull the male pollen producers (stamens) off other flowers of the same species and encase them in plastic bags so they are not fertilized. After a few days, the pollen bags are removed from staminate flowers and are placed on the pistilate flowers, thereby introducing the pollen to the pistils and fertilizing the selected plants.

Activity 47. Planting Trees (4–8)
NSES Science Content Standards

- Unifying concepts and processes in science
- Life science
- Science in personal and social perspectives
- History and nature of science

Additional materials: shovels or trowels, wire mesh

Planting trees can be a great schoolyard activity, but if this is not possible in your location, do not give up. This can also be a good community or volunteer project for a park, environmental center, or reclamation area, or students can raise seedlings on the school grounds and take them home to replant. Because of their value in taking up carbon dioxide and giving off oxygen, trees are very beneficial to the environment, in addition to providing homes and food for many kinds of wildlife. As with any planting project, students should first research native species that will do well in the conditions available around the school or in the selected planting location. Some qualities and needs to consider include mature size; water and nutrient requirements; reproduction (including pollinators and the type of fruit or seeds produced); pollution tolerance; and pests such as viruses, insects, and fungi that might pose a problem for the long-term survival of the tree. Once students are armed with the research to back up their selection, they can draft a proposal for the principal or superintendent explaining why this project will be beneficial for the school. If they are doing a community project instead, students can contact the appropriate community leaders.

Once permission has been received, teams should start growing several trees from seeds or locally harvested seedlings. When the tree seedlings are well established in containers, the students should prepare them for planting outside. If the seedlings have been raised indoors up to this point, they will need to become acclimated to outside temperatures, so they should be moved outside to a location protected from wind and heavy precipitation for a few days. In the meantime, students should prepare the selected planting location on the school grounds and collect the tools needed to loosen the soil and dig a hole. Students can also add some compost as fertilizer, either from classroom waste being composted or from a local garden center. Students should choose the healthiest seedlings and carefully plant them in the prepared locations. The other seedlings can be saved to use as replacements if something happens to the first plants. The trees can be protected from rodents and other animals by enclosing the seedling with a tube of wire mesh or by using plastic and stakes to form a circle around the tree. Students can take pictures as the trees grow and develop, and various groups of students can care for and manage the tree for several years. Over the years, students can record the animals that start to use the tree as a home and can observe seasonal changes and the production of seeds once the tree matures. These activities help create a wonderful ongoing journal of the schoolyard beautification project!

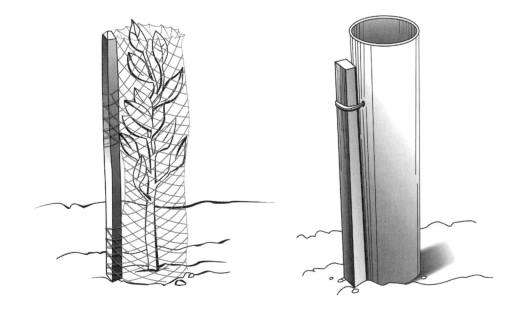

NSES Science Content Standards

- Unifying concepts and processes in science
- Science as inquiry
- Life science
- Earth and space science
- Science in personal and social perspectives
- History and nature of science

Additional materials: plastic pool or tub, or heavy garden or construction plastic (48a); waterproof tape (if needed) (48a)

A garden is an easy and practical area for students to have on the school grounds, but there are other natural areas that can be suitable for development and that will enhance the wildlife habitat in the schoolyard.

a. Creating a pond on the school grounds (4–8)

Nature ponds are a great way to draw a large variety of animals to the schoolyard. Ponds also create ideal areas for native shrubs, herbs, and young trees, which provide the shelters, food sources, and territories for animals the pond will attract. A compost pile covered with chicken wire will also provide shelter and attract prey. The pond will also need a fresh source of water and an outlet to wash away old fluids. If an active stream or spring is not located in the yard, a large water sprinkler can be used. If tap water is used, check with the water company about the chemicals used to treat the water. Often chlorine and fluorine are added to drinking water to destroy aquatic microbes. Since large concentrations of these chemicals could harm the animals attracted to the pond, allow the water to sit in the Sun for several days before using it (pet stores may also carry various chlorine neutralizers). Also, do not use insecticides or herbicides around the pool since they will poison the food of the larger pond creatures.

The pond itself need not be elaborate. It can be as simple as a large children's pool or old laundry tub. It is much more fun, however, for the students to actually design their own pond. Large sheets of plastic used at construction and landscaping sites are perfect for schoolyard ponds since they can be shaped around the students' designs. When obtaining the plastic, which can be found at department or home improvement stores, purchase several rolls of waterproof tape to seal the seams. Students should design the pond to be shallow and provide gently sloping sides for animals to crawl into and out of the pond. Sand and gravel can be used to line the pond. Rocks, logs, branches, and aquatic vegetation (e.g., water lilies) should be placed around the pond for shelter, protection, and preening sites for the animals. The pond should be shaded to prevent the water from getting too hot in the summer. High water temperatures are not good for the animals that will inhabit the pond, especially the insect larva and nymphs that serve as food for the aquatic vertebrates.

Some animals can be antagonistic to one another. If pond plans include fish and frogs, problems can occur, especially if the pond is small. Fish will compete with frogs for oxygen and bugs and will feast on the frog's eggs. If different pond dwellers are desired, students should section the pond into different habitats using screening or an extension of land.

b. Creating a small wildlife sanctuary in the schoolyard (preK–8)

Even if the school is in the center of a town, students can create a small wildlife sanctuary on the school grounds that will attract animals of many types. If students have already constructed a nature pond, they are halfway to making a sanctuary. For organizational purposes, class members should diagram the plot of land where the sanctuary is going to be established so it contains a variety of habitats (sunny lawn, wild hedgerow, small pond, moist woods). Students will be surprised at the many animals—such as birds, rabbits, frogs, and squirrels—that find the little paradise in town over time. Important features for any wildlife sanctuary include four major items. First, there must be shelter for animals and birds, such as trees, shrubs, birdhouses, or brush piles. Another consideration is food for the animals you wish to attract. Feeders and appropriate plants are simple ways to provide a food source. All organisms also need water, so this should be your third consideration. A small pond is ideal, but birdbaths and shallow dishes can also provide water for birds and other animals. Finally, nesting sites help attract birds, insects, and small mammals and keep them in the area. Trees, shrubs, rocks, logs, and birdhouses are some examples of nesting sites. Students can research the animals they can expect to see in their area to make sure they include key elements. Classes can add to the sanctuary each year as they observe which elements seem to attract animals.

Activity 49. Water Baths and Birdhouses (preK–8)
NSES Science Content Standards
- Life science
- Science in personal and social perspectives

Additional materials: metal or plastic-rimmed lids of various sizes (49a), wood and appropriate tools and fasteners (hammers, saws, nails, glue, etc.) (49b), 2 L bottles (49c), straw or grass (49c), a pencil or dowel (49c), scissors or a knife (49c)

Several things can be done to help attract birds and other small animals to the schoolyard. Adding simple baths and houses will undoubtedly improve the diversity of wildlife and the types of animal activities that students can observe.

a. Water baths (preK–8)

If the schoolyard does not have a stream or pond within its boundaries, provide a water bath for the creatures that live there already and for new ones that might be attracted to the school grounds. Water baths need not be expensive; a simple overturned, rimmed lid will work. If the schoolyard has a variety of animals, a large metal or plastic garbage can or barrel lid will suffice. Alternatively, several small lids turned upside-down and filled with clean water and scattered over the grounds allow the animal populations to spread out. Students will immediately notice heavy usage of the makeshift baths. Do not forget that the baths will need to be refilled with clean water each day (a good task for each student to assume periodically).

b. Wood birdhouse (4–8)

Student teams can make an inexpensive birdhouse from scrap wood that is ½–¼ in. thick (the wooden pallets used for moving work well). Students should start the birdhouse by cutting out 7 in. squares to make the back and front sections of the house. Depending on the age and ability of the students, they should either be supervised and follow appropriate safety precautions while using saws, or the pieces should be cut by an adult in advance. An easy way to make a pointed roof is to rotate a square 45 degrees onto one of its tips and use the point at the top for the roof's pitch. Next, students carefully cut long slats of wood 8 in. long by 7 in. wide for the bottom and sides of the birdhouse and make the overhanging slats for the roof 8 in. long and 9 in. wide. For an entrance and perch for the residents, teams should drill a hole in the front square of the house about 1 ⅜ in. round and glue a 3 in. length of wooden dowel into a hole that is a half inch below the entrance hole. Assorted sizes of dowels will work, but make sure to drill a hole that will provide a snug fit for the size of the dowel students are using. Students can add strength and durability to the house by using both 1 in. finishing nails and a high-quality waterproof glue to hold the joints between the sides, ends, and roof together. Teams can add paint or stain to the house to finish. Be sure students let the birdhouses dry thoroughly before setting them up for use.

c. Soda bottle birdhouse (4–8)

A very simple birdhouse can be made from a clean 2 L soda bottle. Students should cut a circular 2 in. hole halfway down the bottle with scissors or a knife for an entrance, then punch a small ⅛ in. hole below the larger one, then insert a pencil firmly to provide a perch for the bird. Next, students punch several drainage holes around the bottom of the bottle and fill the birdhouse with straw or grass up to the pencil. Students should darken the top of the bottle with paint or pull a dark sock down as far as the entrance hole and hang the bottle birdhouse from a tree branch at a slight downward angle so rain does not get into the hole. *Safety note: Caution students to be careful when using scissors or a knife.*

Activity 50. Bird Feeders (preK–8)

NSES Science Content Standards

- Unifying concepts and processes in science
- Life science
- Science in personal and social perspectives

Additional materials: plastic water or soda bottles (50b,c), straws (50b), small socks (50b,c), sugar (50b,c), wide-mouth jar or bottle with lid (50d), small-rimmed dish (50d), milk carton and twigs (50e), coffee can with plastic lid (50f), clothes hangers (50f), wire mesh (50g), drill (50b,f), roofing nail (50b), white vinegar (50b), glue (50b), waterproof glue (50c), large bottle cap (50c), string or wire (50 d), scissors or utility knife (50d,e), large nail (50e,f), eyehook (50f), can opener (50f)

a. Growing flowers to attract hummingbirds (preK–8)

Tiny hummingbirds always generate wonder in children. How can an animal so small have all the body parts of larger birds? Hummingbirds are best seen feeding on trumpet-like flowers, many of which can be grown in a garden around the schoolyard. Since hummingbirds have a poor sense of smell, they compensate with excellent eyesight. Hummingbirds are attracted to flowers with bright, vivid colors, particularly red and orange. Trumpet honeysuckle, bee balm, clematis, fuchsias, hibiscus, phlox, and hollyhocks will attract hummingbirds to the garden.

b. Hummingbird feeders (4–8)

The energy required by hummingbirds is incredible—studies indicate that they must feed every 10 to 15 minutes throughout their waking hours and consume about two-thirds of their body weight in food every day. Sugar is a very important part of their diet, and they get it from nectar and tree sap. In recent years, backyard feeders have become a popular way to help hummingbirds obtain the sugar they need.

One of the easiest hummingbird feeders to make uses a small, disposable water bottle and a few short soda straws. To create the feeder, place an empty bottle snuggly in a red children's sock. Next, drill or create with a roofing nail 8–10 holes through the sock and plastic bottle so a few are on all sides of the container. Force a short piece (¼ in.) of soda straw into each hole so it is tightly enclosed and ring the straw/hole junction with a small amount of glue. Fill the bottle with a rich supply of sugar water, put the lid on the bottle, and hang the setup right-side-up from a low branch of a tree or shrub in the shade so it is at least 4 ft. off the ground.

To make the sugary liquid, mix 1 part sugar with 4 parts water. When making the brew, boil the water first to get rid of pathogens. Do not add food coloring, artificial sweetener, or honey (which will ferment). Also, make sure the feeder is clean by using a white vinegar and water mixture in a 1-to-4 ratio. After the application, make sure the vinegar is completely rinsed from the feeder.

c. Double-lid hummingbird feeder (4–8)

Another type of feeder can be made from the sock-covered water bottle onto which a larger cap (e.g., from a Gatorade bottle) has been glued. In this feeder, several holes are drilled in the water bottle's cap and small beads of waterproof glue (best from a glue gun) are placed near the drilled holes (but not covering them) in two or three locations. Quickly twist short twigs through each drilled hole from the inside of the water bottle cap so they stick out the top about ⅛ in. Press the inside of the larger (Gatorade) cap onto the short ends of the twigs, making sure the bottom of the large cap rests on the beads of glue but does not shut off airflow between it and the small cap. Allow the glue to harden before pulling the twigs through the inside of the cap to open the holes; this should leave a small space for the nutrient-rich liquid to flow between the two caps. Fill the water bottle with sugar nectar and screw it onto the smaller lid. Hang the feeder upside down from a limb of a small tree or shrub in the shade so it is at least 4 ft. off the ground.

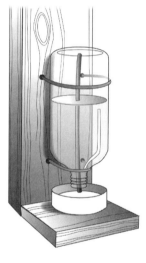

d. Common bird feeder made from a bottle and dish (preK–8)

Have students fill a large-mouth plastic jar or bottle with bird seed. Using a knife or scissors, cut holes in the lid large enough for the seed to pass through easily, put on the lid, invert the bottle, and suspend the setup above a rimmed dish or large plastic lid, leaving a ½ in. gap between the bottle's lid and the dish. The bottle can be suspended by taping a string to the bottom securely or by poking two small holes in the plastic jar or bottle and inserting string or wire before filling the container with birdseed. Alternatively, students can cut small holes in the sides of bottle near the bottom and suspend the feeder over a dish by tying string around the neck of a bottle so that birds can peck into the bottom to release the seeds.

e. Common bird feeder made from a milk carton (preK–3)

Milk carton feeders are easy and inexpensive to make and remarkably effective for keeping bird seed dry. The feeders attract finches, sparrows, chickadees, and other small birds. To create the feeder, students start by outlining the feeding opening in the front of the carton. This opening should resemble the feeder itself with a peaked roof. Students can use scissors to cut the openings, or this can be done by the teacher in advance for younger children. While cutting the opening, students need to leave about 3 in. of carton above the opening (before the carton begins to fold inward to create the pour spout); 1 in. of carton should remain on each side and 2 in. of carton should remain at the bottom. The paper section cut from the carton can be fashioned into a roof and attached with tape or glue to protect the insides of the opening from foul weather. Students will need to find several sturdy twigs to act as perches for the birds and secure them to the lower front section of the carton by pushing the twigs into holes (created by a large nail) deep into and out the back of the carton. Birdseed is placed in the opening to rest on the bottom of the feeder.

f. Common bird feeder made from a coffee can (preK–3)

A coffee can feeder is one of the simplest and easiest bird feeding stations to make. Students cleanly remove one metal end of a 13 oz. coffee can (retaining its plastic top). With younger students, the teacher may want to remove the metal end before starting the project. Cut a large semicircle (half a circle) opening in the plastic lid, leaving an inch of plastic around the hole so the lid's rim isn't damaged. The hole should be large enough for the bird to move into the can if it desires. Students can hang the can feeder sideways from a tree branch using an unwrapped clothes hanger that has had the ends poked into the can (through holes made by a nail).

g. Suet bird feeders (4–8)

Most birds love to peck at the white fat or lard known as suet that comes from meats and meat products (e.g., bacon fat). Because their diet generally consists of low-fat foods such as seeds and insects, birds need to supplement their diets with fats. Students can easily make a number of different types of suet feeders. They can roll a ball or fashion a cake of lard and place it on a dish or rock (often called a mutton ball or cake).

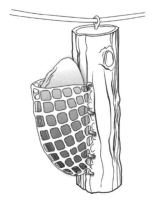

Another effective, easy-to-make feeder has students shape the wire mesh so it forms a basket that can hold suet and tack it on a block of wood (leaving the top open to refill the feeder). They can screw a small eye hook into the top of the block to hang the feeder from a tree branch. Alternatively, students can balloon out two squares of wire mesh screening and lace them together along the sides and bottom with wire or twine to create a pocket (leaving the top open for refilling), then hang it from a tree branch using a short wire that is attached to the back screen. Finally, students can drill several inch-deep holes in a small log, stuff suet into the holes, and hang the log feeder on a tree limb.

7 Insects and Other Invertebrates

Activity 51. A Closer Look at Diversity in Invertebrate Animals (preK–8)

NSES Science Content Standards

- Unifying concepts and processes in science
- Science as inquiry
- Life science

Topic: Invertebrates
Go to: www.scilinks.org
Code: SYS022

Additional materials: magnifying glasses

As with plants, invertebrate animals demonstrate tremendous diversity. Listed below are several examples of invertebrates easily observed around a schoolyard. *Remind students not to look at the Sun with magnifying glasses.* Challenges that can be presented to student groups include the following:

1. Locate five earthworms in leaf piles within the schoolyard. With a bit of looking, students should be able to find three very different sizes of worms. These are actually three different species: top dwellers found less than 3 in. deep (small size), middle dwellers found 3–6 in. deep (medium size), and lower dwellers found more than 6 in. deep (large size). Students should compare the worms they find, looking for similarities and differences.

2. Locate five different types of insects. An abundant number of insects exist in a schoolyard, but most try to remain out of view of predatory animals (e.g., birds). Once five are found, students can compare their anatomies and find three different characteristics and three common characteristics.

3. Locate five different butterflies on the school grounds and compare their body and head anatomies, colors, and wing patterns.

4. Locate five different bugs that are not insects (have more than six legs). Despite the fact that they are often found in the same location, not all small organisms (arthropods) found in the schoolyard are insects. Once students locate an organism, they should record and sketch it in their nature journal.

5. Locate five different types of spiders on the school grounds. This activity can also be done with different colors or sizes of spiders.

6. Locate three different mollusks in the schoolyard and compare different features. This is a difficult one unless there is a lake or pond near the school. However, a few varieties of land snails and slugs can generally be located on school grounds.

7. Locate five different types of invertebrate animal homes. Students really enjoy looking for invertebrate homes, and the activity on spiderweb capture (Activity 15, pp. 25–26) can be helpful.

Activity 52. Observing Insects (preK–8)

NSES Science Content Standards

- Unifying concepts and processes in science
- Science as inquiry
- Life science

Topic: Insects
Go to: *www.scilinks.org*
Code: SYS023

Additional materials: magnifying glasses

Students will need to watch for bugs invading vegetation around the school. When a bug is observed, team members should watch it for 5 or 10 minutes to "learn its ways" (how it moves, what it eats, how it defends itself, what habitat it lives in). After a period of behavioral observation, the bug should be caught in a small jar for study, identification, and sketching in the nature journal at the rendezvous or resource site. Magnifying lenses can also be used to examine features of the insect more closely. Bugs should be set free after they are studied. Each student or team should have the opportunity to observe at least four different insects. *Remind students not to look at the Sun with magnifying glasses.*

Activity 53. Collecting, Rearing, and Experimenting With Flatworms (4–8)

NSES Science Content Standards

- Unifying concepts and processes in science
- Science as inquiry
- Life science

Additional materials: magnifying glasses, organ meat for bait, gloves

A flatworms is very different from a roundworm in that it does not have a cylindrical shape and segmented body. There are a number of flatworms; some are parasites and others are nonparasitic. In this activity, students try to capture one of the most prevalent of the nonparasitic flatworms, called *planaria* (singular form is *planarian*). These worms are readily captured on fresh, soft organ meats such as liver or spleen, which you place in a nonpolluted lake or stream for several days. Students must come up with a way to retrieve the bait without getting wet, as the meat should be placed under water slightly away from the edge. Once this is figured out, students should find several planaria crawling over and then ingesting the meat; they can carry the planaria in some water to the school grounds for observation and experimentation.

After a break of several hours to allow the planaria to settle, students can examine the flatworm's anatomy with a magnifying glass. One of the first things they will note is that there are two eye spots at the front end of the worm, each one pointing to the other. This creates the impression that they are cross-eyed, which does not affect the worm at all because a planarian's eyes see only cloudy dark and light images (students may be challenged to come up with an experiment to see if the worms favor or do not favor light). Because of the eye pattern, however, the planarian is sometimes known as the cross-eyed worm. Other features can be readily seen under magnification. From a mass of nerves between the eye, nerve cords can be seen descending the right and left sides of the body, connected to one another by transverse nerves. Tubular kidneys lie along the sides of the worm, and a central mouth and throat occupy the center of the body.

One of the most remarkable feats of the planarian is the ability to regenerate parts of the anatomy that are injured or destroyed. The process is known as *regeneration*. Students may want to experiment with this phenomenon by separating the body of a planarian in two and keeping records of the regeneration process during the healing. *Remind students not to look at the Sun with magnifying glasses. Always handle raw meat with gloves.*

Activity 54. Studying Worms and Creating a Worm Habitat (preK–8)

NSES Science Content Standards

- Unifying concepts and processes in science
- Science as inquiry
- Life science

Additional materials: jars or bottles of different sizes

Topic: Worms
Go to: www.scilinks.org
Code: SYS024

Students of all ages like this activity because it allows them to see what happens with the worms that live in the schoolyard's soil. Find two different-size clean jars or soda bottles (remove the top at the neck of the soda bottles if you use them). Place the smaller bottle inside the first so that there is about an inch of space between the two all the way around. Worms need air, so if you are going to put tops on the jars, make sure you drill several holes in the lids. Fill the space between the two jars with topsoil that you have mixed with an even mix of sand, coffee grounds, and oatmeal. Be careful not to overfill the unit with soil; leave about 2 in. at the top. Add enough water to make the soil moist but not saturated, and add torn-up grass, twigs, and dead leaves on the soil, leaving about an inch of space from the top. Find several earthworms around the schoolyard (check under leaves, rocks, and rotting wood) and place them on the leaf debris on top of the soil. Cover the setup loosely with a lid or cloth secured with a rubber band. Cover the jars with dark material so the worms are in darkness. Place the worm settlement in a safe, protected place on the school grounds. The habitat should be observed frequently by briefly removing the dark cover to make sure the soil stays moist.

As the students collect worms around the school grounds, they will notice three different-size worms. They may find small, skinny worms that feed and live at the surface of the soil; medium-size worms that feed and live 3–6 in. from the top of the soil; and large worms that reside in the deeper areas of the soil. The three different-size worms are different species, not just worms growing from infants to adults.

Activity 55. Studying the Movements of Slugs and Snails (preK–8)

NSES Science Content Standards
- Unifying concepts and processes in science
- Science as inquiry
- Life science

*SCI*LINKS.
THE WORLD'S A CLICK AWAY

Topic: Mollusks
Go to: *www.scilinks.org*
Code: SYS025

Additional materials: magnifying glasses, mirrors or glass plates

Have your students ever wondered how an animal without feet can move? When you ask them, they may respond with "wings" or "fins." But if they are asked how animals can move on land without feet, they generally are stumped. This sets up the perfect introduction to the movements of mollusks, primarily snails. To move, a snail secretes mucus from glands near its mouth and slides its body along on the sticky film. The film takes on a silvery sheen once in contact with air. This can be seen easily when one watches a slug or snail creep along a surface. Slugs and snails can usually be found under branches or rocks in the schoolyard. Once they are found, have students observe the snail's movement across a smooth surface or wrapped along a rough surface such as a branch. If a mirror is handy, students can actually see the snail secreting the mucus from its mucus glands. The real treat, however, comes from watching from below as a slug or snail slides along a clear glass plate. From this vantage point, students will see not only the secretion release but also the rhythmic, ripplelike movements of the muscles in the "foot" of the mollusk. It is also fun for students to place dull or sharp obstacles in front of the snail and watch it slide over, or have a race to see whose mollusk is the fastest.

Activity 56. Capturing Invertebrates From Soils (preK–8)

NSES Science Content Standards
- Unifying concepts and processes in science
- Science as inquiry
- Life science

Additional materials: funnels or inverted soda bottles with the bottom removed, scouring pad or fine mesh screen, coffee can, dish soap or vinegar, magnifying glass

Students of all ages can benefit from this activity. Teams collect soils (accompanied with leaf and grass litter) from various locations around the schoolyard, making sure to note location, color, moisture, and texture of each sample in their field report. Students

loosely place the soil and grass litter in a large bottle that has had its bottom removed (e.g., 2 L soda bottle) or a large funnel. To keep the soil debris from falling through the funnel, students should set a small piece of scouring pad or fine mesh screen at the neck. They then place the bottle upside-down in a coffee can so that the neck of the bottle is about 2 in. off the bottom of the can. To prevent critters that fall into the can from escaping, students should pour an inch of diluted dish soap or vinegar into the coffee can. To make sure the bottle will sit upside-down for several days without falling, teams should tape the bottle to the can. Alternatively, the container can be set in a hole in the ground so that organisms will fall in as they walk along. Either way, leave the setup in a protected area in the schoolyard for several days, where it can be in the sunlight for much of the time. After several days, students should remove the soda bottle and funnel and pour the liquid with the captured creatures into a shallow dish, where they can be examined with a magnifying glass or hand lens.

Critters that might be caught would include tiny animals that will need to be magnified and larger critters such as centipedes, millipedes, spiders, mites, larva, and nematode worms, which are seen easily without magnification.

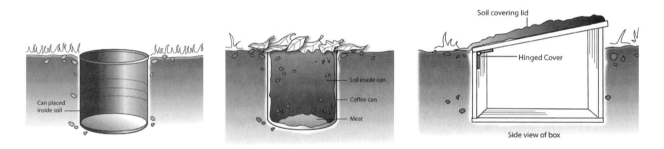

Activity 57. Capturing Invertebrates in Shallow Streams and Ponds (4–8)

NSES Science Content Standards

- Unifying concepts and processes in science
- Science as inquiry
- Life science

Topic: Invertebrates
Go to: *www.scilinks.org*
Code: SYS022

Additional materials: strainers or nets, jars and pans, flotation devices

Students usually love to investigate shallow streams and ponds, but doing so can be messy. The appropriate gear will make this activity much easier. Also, water exploration brings with it the danger of drowning, so extra precautions (i.e., providing additional adult supervisors and flotation devices) need to be taken. A fast-moving, shallow stream that travels through the schoolyard will work beautifully for this activity. Working in teams, students can find invertebrates in streams by checking under rocks, branches, and plant debris. They can also use large kitchen strainers and fine-meshed nets to catch invertebrates swept into the stream's current when a teammate dislodges a rock just upstream from the netlike trap. When students discover an invertebrate, they can transfer it into a small, covered jar half-filled with water for observation, identification, and notation in their nature journals. Pond studies are most productive when teams check the vegetation and sand or mud along the shallow borders of the pond.

> Invertebrates that are most commonly found in streams and ponds include the insect larvae and nymphs of mayflies, stoneflies, caddisflies, dobsonflies, water beetles, and dragonflies. Adult insects such as water boatman, backswimmers, water scorpions, water beetles, water striders, and diving beetles can also be found, along with noninsect arthropods such as crayfish, scuds, mites, and shrimp. Additional invertebrates such as clams; mussels; snails; water pennies; and round, flat, and segmented worms are also generally found.

Activity 58. Trapping an Insect for Study (preK–8)

NSES Science Content Standards

- Unifying concepts and processes in science
- Science as inquiry
- Life science
- Science and technology

Additional materials: netting, 2 L plastic soda bottle, sweet liquid (e.g., leftover soda), duct tape, plastic tubing

It is sometimes beneficial for teachers to encourage student teams to capture a schoolyard insect for in-depth exploration. Catching an insect can be frustrating, but there are several easy, safe traps that students can make to snare a bug.

Topic: Insects
Go to: *www.scilinks.org*
Code: SYS023

- *Parachute net trap:* This trap can be made from lightweight netting commonly found at craft shops or fabric stores. The trap resembles a large net parachute with a drawstring around its perimeter. When students find an insect they wish to study, the trap is placed around the large section of plant holding the insect and the drawstring is tightened around the branches and leaves on which the insect is resting. With the bug inside the net bag with plenty of food (the plant) to eat, it can be studied for several days. (This trap is not recommended for butterflies or voracious predatory insects.)

- *Soda bottle trap:* A 2 L soda bottle with some sweet liquid (leftover soda) works especially well to catch insects (particularly flying insects) that love sweets. Cut off the top of the bottle with scissors or a knife (make sure that students are properly supervised) where the neck expands and turn the cut edges into the bottle so they point toward the bottom; cover the cut edges with duct tape. Place the bottle on its side in an out-of-the-way location in the garden with its opening low to the ground. Insects will be attracted to the sweet soda and will walk or fly inside; once they are in, they will not be able to get out!

- *Bottle-tubing trap:* Clean out a 2 L soda bottle and poke two or three holes at different spots around the middle of the bottle. The holes should be the same size as a short length of plastic tubing, approximately ½ in. diameter. Cut the tubing into short pieces (about 6 in.) and insert the pieces in the holes pointing toward the ground, leaving most of the tube outside the bottle. Pour a bit of soda or sugar water in the upright bottle. Flies will enter the tubes to get to the sugar but will be unable to find their way back out.

- *Slug and beetle trap:* This trap is easy and fun to construct. Using scissors or a knife (make sure to supervise students), cut out a series of 1 in. windows around the midsection of a 2 L bottle so they are all the same height from the bottom of the bottle. Bury the bottle in soil up to the level of the bottom of the windows and pour about ½ in. of soda into the bottle. Cap the bottle to keep out twigs and rain. Slugs and beetles are attracted to the fluids but are not able to escape.

Activity 59. Cover Board Invertebrate Studies (preK–8)

NSES Science Content Standards

- Unifying concepts and processes in science
- Life science

Additional materials: 12 in. × 12 in. squares of untreated plywood, permanent markers for numbering the boards, magnifying glasses, forceps, small jars or containers

Cover boards are an easy way to create artificial habitats to study invertebrates. Many types of insects, millipedes, centipedes, worms, and assorted other invertebrates prefer to live in dark, damp places. A cover board will provide these things and can be easily moved to study the organisms that have taken refuge underneath. To use cover boards, simply identify locations in various habitats and clear away all leaf litter and debris from the area where the board will be placed. The cover board should be placed directly on the soil. Depending on the space available, the cover boards can be placed in a transect (a straight line) or an array (a grid with boards evenly spaced 3–5 m apart). Number each board to make data collection easier. Once cover boards are in place, they can be left indefinitely. For safety, students should always stand behind the boards and pull the far edge back toward themselves when moving them to make observations. Replace the boards once everything has been completed so they are ready for the next time.

Younger students may use the cover boards to compare invertebrates in different habitats or to compare the diversity found under each board. Older students can make predictions about diversity, habitats, seasonal changes, specific groups of organisms (decomposers, predatory insects, and so forth) and can collect data over several weeks or months. Students use graphing and data analysis to evaluate their information. They can also research the organisms they find, learning about trophic levels, species interactions, and food chains in a microhabitat.

Activity 60. Studying Ants and Creating an Ant Habitat (preK–8)

NSES Science Content Standards
- Unifying concepts and processes in science
- Science as inquiry
- Life science

Additional materials: clear jars with lids in different sizes, small nails, hammer, implement for digging (spoon, trowel, small shovel)

Many students may be curious about what an ant nest looks like under the soil in the schoolyard. To find out, locate two tall but different-size clean jars with tightly fitting lids (e.g., different-size peanut butter jars). Students punch holes in the larger lid, making sure the holes are smaller than the ants. Students place the smaller jar in the larger jar, maintaining about an inch of space between the inner and the outer jars all the way around the setup. Find an active ant nest somewhere in the schoolyard and dig carefully into the nest to capture several worker ants, the queen ant (often with wings), ant larva, and ant eggs. Roll a piece of paper into a funnel and pour a bit of the soil not containing the ants into the space between the two jars. Next, carefully pour the ants, eggs, and larva onto the soil and immediately screw on the lids of both jars. The worker ants will immediately start to dig tunnels and move the larva and queen to safety under the soil. Because ants build their nests underground, the students need to darken the setup with a cover thick enough to keep out the sunshine when the ants are not being observed.

When the ants have settled (after about 10 minutes), students should feed the ants a small amount of honey or sugar-soaked bread and tiny bits of fruits and vegetables. They should also place a cotton ball soaked with water away from the food so it does not encourage the growth of mold. Members of the class should resupply the ants with food every few days. Once the ant colony is established, it can be left in a secure and sheltered area of the schoolyard. Care must be taken that the ant habitat is not shaken or disturbed too much so the tunnels and rearing areas are not destroyed.

Activity 61. Spittle Bugs (preK–8)
NSES Science Content Standards
- Unifying concepts and processes in science
- Science as inquiry
- Life science

Spittle bugs are very interesting to children of all ages because of the insect's habit of covering itself with a copious amount of bubbly fluid that resembles spit while the insect rests on a plant (generally in unmowed areas of school grounds). The nymph of the bug produces the fluid from juices it extracts from the plant and uses the bubbles to conceal itself from predators. The nymph can be easily discovered by pushing aside the spittle to reveal the large false eyes protruding from the base of two flightless wings. Eventually the nymph will grow into a ½ in. long leaf hopper–type insect.

Activity 62. Racing Harvestmen or Daddy Longlegs (preK–8)
NSES Science Content Standards
- Unifying concepts and processes in science
- Science as inquiry
- Life science

"Have you ever heard that daddy longlegs are one of the most poisonous spiders, but their fangs are too short to bite humans?" The statement is false; the common daddy longlegs found throughout most of North America is harmless. The confusion may lie with true, long-legged spiders found primarily in the Pacific Coast and in the southwest desert regions. These true spiders have two body segments, spin a web of silk, and have small hollow fanglike teeth, but they are not highly poisonous. The common North American daddy longlegs has a single-segmented, pill-like body with a pair of eyes on the front end and on the side, and eight incredibly long legs (sometimes more than an inch long). However, they are not true spiders (they belong in the order Opiliones), do not spin a web of silk, and are only found in webs when being eaten by true spiders. They are generally found under logs in woodpiles, sheds, and other places where the humidity is high. Daddy longlegs feed on small, soft-bodied insects, but many also feed on plant juices.

It is often fun to catch daddy longlegs and see which ones move the fastest. This is usually done by marking a large circle (15 ft. diameter) on a bare surface, such as a parking lot or playground, and placing the daddy longlegs in the center of the circle. This works best if each student has only one daddy longlegs to observe. When released, the insect will run instantly toward the perimeter of the circle. Races can also be developed up a wall or around a circular track.

A similar activity includes obstacles that are placed in front of the daddy longlegs as it races toward the perimeter of a circle. Students draw increasingly larger, concentric circles within the large circle (like a target) and place on each circle specific obstacles, such as tree branches, blocks of wood, or large rocks. Students should work in teams for this activity.

Activity 63. Observing and Experimenting With Isopods: Sow Bugs and Pill Bugs (preK–8)

NSES Science Content Standards
- Unifying concepts and processes in science
- Science as inquiry
- Life science

Additional materials: magnifying glass

Students love to work with these little arthropods and are sometimes surprised to learn they are not insects. Isopods are water-loving crustaceans and are easily found in the schoolyard by turning over logs or rocks, looking under freshly watered flower pots, or digging through the soil where wood is decomposing. Often described as a baby armadillo (it is not), the little bug (especially a pill bug) tends to roll into a tight ball to hide its soft underside and expose its hard exoskeleton when threatened. Sow bugs are not able to roll up as tightly as pill bugs. Both species of these crustaceans mate throughout the year, and the females carry the eggs, numbering around 100, in a brood pouch on the undersides of their bodies. In many ways, the structural features of the two are actually quite distinctive. Challenge student teams to locate both kinds of bugs and, after observing them carefully, come up with three differences between the two kinds of organisms. *Remind students not to look at the Sun with magnifying glasses.*

- *Experimenting with isopods:* Because pill bugs and sow bugs are harmless and do not carry diseases students can catch, they are perfect animals for an activity. Questions concerning moisture, sound, light, smell, food, and substrate levels are

> The bodies of sow bugs are flat and elongated, and they possess well-developed eyes, seven pairs of legs, and overlapping "armored" plates. They have two tail-like appendages on their rear ends and tend to move more quickly than pill bugs. Pill bugs are slimmer and are not as flat as sow bugs, and they do not have the tail-like structures. Pill bugs move a bit more slowly than sow bugs and are much better than their counterparts are at rolling up into a tight ball.

easy to set up. Challenge student teams to come up with a hypothesis to test in a controlled science experiment with pill bugs and sow bugs in the schoolyard.

- *Comparing similarities of isopods and other land arthropods:* Students might not realize the incredible diversity in arthropods, the jointed leg invertebrates. All creatures in this phylum have exoskeletons surrounding their bodies and have similar body systems, sensing apparatuses, and reproductive mechanisms. All the appendages coming off their bodies are jointed, so they can flex and extend the limbs. Challenge teams to list in a short time period as many different animals as they can that fit into this category.

- *Examining differences between isopods and other land arthropods:* This exercise is a bit trickier than the earlier comparison of pill bugs and sow bugs because students are now being asked to compare just isopods with other arthropods. Challenge student teams to list as many isopod characteristics as they can think of that are different from each of the arthropods described previously.

Activity 64. Examining Insect Galls (preK–8)
NSES Science Content Standards

- Unifying concepts and processes in science
- Science as inquiry
- Life science

Additional materials: magnifying glass

Students often question what the large, rounded growths on plant stems or leaves are; they are usually surprised by the answer. The growths are called *galls,* which are produced by the plant itself in response to the feeding or egg-laying of certain insects. When an insect punctures a plant to feed or lay an egg, it gives off chemicals that cause the plant to grow around the insect. The growth encapsulates the insect or eggs in an effort to alleviate the irritant. When this is done, however, the insect or its eggs become protected from weather and predators for a long period of time. Galls can be either hard (like the galls on the stems of goldenrod) or papery (like the "oak apples" formed by oak trees). Different insects cause galls to form throughout the year, particularly in the spring on maple and oak trees and in the summer and fall on hackberry trees. Generally, more than one larva is inside each gall.

Challenge student teams to locate at least three different types of galls growing on plants in the schoolyard. Once a team has found three types, its members can cut open the galls to observe the developing insect. Usually the developing insect larvae will be from a fly, wasp, beetle, or moth. The four are easy to tell apart with a magnifying glass. Fly larvae do not have an obvious head or legs and will move very infrequently; wasp larvae also show no obvious head or legs and stay very still, but they show a very small, narrow, pinlike structure at the end of their abdomen; and moth larvae have a head and legs and will usually move quite a bit, while beetle larvae will have a delicate pair of horns that rise from the front part of their tiny head.

Although many galls are produced by plants in the autumn, they can be collected at any time for larvae examination in the fall, winter, and spring (by summer, the larvae have usually emerged). It is usually great fun for students to bring galls to school whenever they find them to investigate immediately, but galls can also be stored in covered containers until the insect emerges in the spring. Once the insect emerges, it may be difficult to distinguish because of its small size, so magnification may be required. Some insects that develop in galls through the winter are colored a bright metallic blue or green or have especially long protrusions that can be seen easily without much enlarging.

Activity 65. Observing Insect Metamorphosis (preK–8)
NSES Science Content Standards
- Unifying concepts and processes in science
- Science as inquiry
- Life science

Additional materials: magnifying glasses

It is interesting for students to raise insects from eggs found in the autumn or winter on the underside of leaves, twigs, and bark or buried in leaf litter or the ground. If eggs are discovered, students should not dislodge them but should bring as much of the substance holding the eggs as possible to a designated location in the schoolyard where they can be observed easily using a magnifying glass. Sometimes the eggs have hatched into worm- or grublike larvae earlier and grown over the summer. Other times, the eggs lie dormant at the site. With the coming of freezing weather, the fully fed larvae may have spun cocoons in which they spend the winter and usually transform into a pupa. With warm weather and the longer length of spring days, the insects in the cocoon or egg speed their development and prepare to emerge from their winter shelter. Insects that emerge resembling a miniature adult are called *nymphs* (e.g., grasshoppers), eat rapidly, and grow into an adult. Insects that emerge from the egg as larva begin to devour food as quickly as possible and grow rapidly, preparing to go into their pupa stage (cocoon) by midsummer. Those that have spent the winter in a cocoon as pupa emerge in the adult form. That being said, insect metamorphosis can go from egg to nymph to adult (called *incomplete metamorphosis*) or from egg to larva to pupa to adult (called *complete metamorphosis*). Challenge student teams to locate insects in the schoolyard that go through both types of life cycles.

Migrate away from the area. Migration is the strategy of leaving the region and flying to warmer climates as the weather becomes cold in the autumn. The monarch butterfly is a well-known example, flying from North America to the tropics in the fall and returning in the spring. Many crop insect pests migrate south for the winter as well.

Overwinter as eggs. Some insects lay eggs in protective encasements to withstand the cold temperatures of winter. The praying mantis is well known for this.

Overwinter as larvae. Larvae are the wormlike form of insects that hatch from eggs during metamorphosis. As cold weather approaches, the larvae of some types of insects burrow into the leaf litter (e.g., woolly bear caterpillars) or dig deep into loose soil (e.g., grubs). Some spend the winter in galls (swellings in plant tissues), and others, such as wood-boring beetles, chew their way deep into tree wood. Sometimes the larvae store huge amounts of glycerol, a component of fat molecules, in their body fluids, which serves as a type of antifreeze.

Overwinter as pupae. As noted in the metamorphosis activity, a pupa is the mummylike stage of development in which the insect is transformed from a larva to an adult. Usually the pupae are attached to the food the adults will consume after they emerge. The best examples of this strategy are the luna moth and cecropia moth.

Overwinter as nymphs. Nymphs are young insects that resemble their larger parents. Usually, nymphs survive under water in streams and ponds, eating decomposing leaves or small aquatic animals and breathing with primitive gills. Many of the macroinvertebrates discussed elsewhere in this book are excellent examples.

Overwinter by slowing all body functions. There are many adult insects that go into a state of suspended dormancy in winter called *diapause*—similar to hibernation in mammals. Usually insects that follow this strategy store increased levels of glycerol in their body fluids, which acts like antifreeze to prevent ice formation. Many hibernating adults survive in hollow trees and under bark or rocks. Ladybugs and solitary wasps are good examples of insects that follow this strategy.

Overwinter by clustering and heat generation. Social insect populations generally use this strategy of making it through the winter by becoming semiactive, staying huddled in their hives and generating heat by moving their appendages. Honeybees are the best-known examples of this strategy. Studies have found that honeybees consume 20–25 lbs. of honey during the winter months and create heat by oxidizing the sugars. The clustered bees circulate the heat around themselves by fanning their wings.

a. Providing a site that encourages insects to lay eggs or go into dormancy (preK–8)

This is an easy way to see what happens as insects prepare for cold weather or a change in their growth stage. Remove the cap from an empty 2 L soda bottle and cut a vertical ¼ in. slit halfway to the bottom. Place the bottle in the bushes or under a stone or wood pile. Insects will be attracted to the bottle because of the shelter and dormancy space provided for overwintering.

b. How do insects survive the winter? (preK–8)

Students often wonder how insects survive through the cold of winter. There are many answers to this question since insects use a variety of methods to survive the winter months. The severity of the winter, the frequent alternating of thaws and freezes, and the thickness of snow cover often impact insect survival. Listed below are a number of insect survival strategies. *Remind students not to look at the Sun with magnifying glasses.*

8 Studying Vertebrates

Activity 66. A Closer Look at Diversity in Vertebrate Animals (preK–8)

NSES Science Content Standards

- Unifying concepts and processes in science
- Science as inquiry
- Life science

Additional materials: net to catch fish

Topic: Vertebrates
Go to: *www.scilinks.org*
Code: SYS027

Vertebrate animals can also be found in the schoolyard, especially if a stream or pond is located on the property. Even if a stream or pond is not present, students may be able to find toads, snakes, and birds on the grounds, especially in the less-attended areas around the school. Make sure that all organisms are released once the activities are finished. In this activity, challenge students to:

1. Locate and attempt to catch with a net three different fish in a stream or pond and research the identification and niche of each. This exercise requires taking the class to a stream or pond, which may not be available on the school grounds. As an alternative, students could explore a stream or pond as a team on a weekend and bring the fish they catch (in a container filled with water) to school on Monday to share. If more than three fish are caught, they can be put together in a children's pool and each team can research a single species. Teachers should make sure they check local fishing regulations before having students catch fish. *Use appropriate safety precautions around water, including flotation devices and additional supervision if needed.*

2. Locate and attempt to catch three different amphibians on the grounds. This activity can be accomplished on the schoolyard if shaded, moist areas are on the property.

3. Locate and attempt to catch three different reptiles in the schoolyard. Similar to the exercise above, reptiles can be found in the less-visited areas on the school grounds.

4. Try to spot five different types of birds in the schoolyard. There should be no problem accomplishing this fun task.

Activity 67. Establishing Feeding and Defecation Stations (preK–8)

NSES Science Content Standards

- Unifying concepts and processes in science
- Science as inquiry
- Life science
- Science in personal and social perspectives

Additional materials: wire or string, nails, etc. for securing feeding stations

In addition to placing feeders in the schoolyard to attract birds, there are ways to increase the likelihood that other animals will wander in on a regular basis. Feeding stations for other animals may increase the wildlife spotted on the school grounds. Defecation stations will also provide evidence that the animals passed through the area, even if they were not observed. *Remind students not to touch or handle animal waste.*

a. Feeding stations for animals (preK–8)

Creating places for animals to feed around the school grounds is fun and educationally enlightening for students. Feeding stations are particularly useful in the winter and spring, when the natural foods of many regions are scarce. Making food available at these lean times is critical for many of nature's creatures because it will determine whether certain animals will survive to reproduce or die.

Animals often like to eat on flat surfaces, and many prefer to feed above the ground, where they have a clearer view of their surroundings. One of the easiest types of feeding boards to provide in a schoolyard is a 2 ft. high tree trunk cut cleanly across the top surface, which provides a clear, flat surface for the animal to sit on while feeding.

The type of food used in feeding stations varies widely. Unshelled and succulent foods are short-lived and will spoil quickly if the temperature in the environment climbs above the freezing mark. Shelled and dried foods last much longer but require a good supply of water if eaten in any quantity. To prevent animals from carrying away and hoarding food, students can fasten foods like ear corn or berry branches to objects in the area or secure them to spikes driven into the ground, nails pounded into boards, or wires wrapped around branches or trees. Smaller foods such as nuts or acorns can be placed in small mesh wire baskets or boxes so animals can remove the nuts with difficulty. It is important to remember that once a feeding station is established, it should be continuously supplied with food for the remainder of the season.

b. Scat boards (preK–8)

Interestingly, animals generally like to deposit their wastes on a smooth surface, such as along a well-beaten path, on a beach, or in a short grass meadow. This provides an excellent opportunity for students to study scat variation in nature by placing a series of smooth surfaces, called scat boards, around the schoolyard one day and checking the surfaces the following day. Scat boards are easily made by cutting out 9–12 in. squares of plywood (or using individual floor tiles) and placing them in a sampling area. This activity is great for team research projects, such as investigating whether color, pattern design, board shape, construction material, and location are important in attracting animals.

Despite the fact that all scat is made of indigestible waste from different animals, it varies considerably in shape, size, and internal microscopic and macroscopic ingredients. Rabbit scat, for example, is brown and spherical, while fox scat is black, cylindrical, and pointed at either end. The differences in size, shape, and sometimes odor allow naturalists to identify the specific kind of animal that dropped the scat on the ground. When found in nature or on smooth scat boards around the school, students can sketch the scat (its size and shape) in their nature journal, then later in the day check the identification of the scat varieties they observed. Scat boards should be disposed of by incineration to destroy bacteria or parasites that may be present.

Activity 68. Safely Trapping Animals (4–8)

NSES Science Content Standards

- Unifying concepts and processes in science
- Life science
- Science and technology
- Science in personal and social perspectives

Additional materials: gloves, 2 qt. glass mason jar, screw-on ring, stiff wire, tin can lid, drill, pliers, empty coffee can, mouse trap, screen, mesh fence or hadrware cloth, plywood

Preparing for this activity can be difficult because there is a lot of potential for variety of organisms that might be found in a schoolyard. In addition, because animals tend to move around a lot, it is often difficult to estimate their abundance, range, and frequency. On the other hand, most animals tend to reveal their presence through trails, footprints, droppings, sounds, remains, and homes. Well-prepared student teams will find it exciting and rewarding to devise ways to observe and capture animals on the school grounds. A number of accurate and safe ways to observe and capture small animals in a schoolyard are noted below. Remember, however, when working with any nondomesticated animal, students should wear gloves and must handle the animals carefully so as not to be bitten or harm the animal. Also, most states have laws prohibiting keeping animals caught in nature; if animals are trapped in the schoolyard, they must all be released back onto the school grounds after being observed. Check to be sure that your area does not have laws prohibiting the capture of small rodents.

- *Horne jar trap:* A Horne jar trap can be made from a 2 qt. glass mason jar, a screw-on ring that fits the jar, a stiff wire, and the lid of a tin can. Two holes are drilled into the top edge of the rim of the screw-on ring 2–3 in. apart, and a stiff wire is inserted into the holes and bent at each end; this wire will hold the tin can lid door in place. A door that loosely fits the opening of the jar is cut from the lid of the tin can using tin snips or heavy scissors and then bent over the wire at one end. Pliers work well for bending this piece. This door will swing open into the jar, fall back into place over the jar mouth, and

catch on the inside edge of the screw-on ring, which prevents it from swinging out, thus capturing the animal inside. Food is placed in the jar to attract animals, and the trap is set horizontally along an active runway where small animals might travel.

- *Coffee-can trap:* A coffee-can trap can be made from an empty coffee can screwed onto a short, flat board to prevent the can from rolling. The screw also attaches a mouse trap through the lip of the can into the board so that the guillotine of the trap flaps inward. To the guillotine, a stout, square screen is lashed with short lengths of wire. The screen must be large enough to stop the guillotine from flopping past the mouth of the coffee can and into the trap 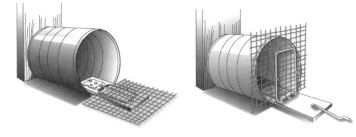 injuring the animal. When a piece of bait is placed on the trigger of the cocked guillotine, the trap is set.

- *Funnel trap:* Another trap can easily be made with a length of fine mesh fence or hardware cloth held in place with stakes of wire from an old coat hanger. This creates a pathway that guides an animal into the trap (see the diagram below). At each end of this trap, the wire screening is shaped to resemble a funnel, ending in a small hole that leads the animal into a small screened 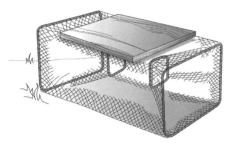 box. An opening to remove the captive is at the top of the box and is covered with a piece of plywood to prevent escape. A rock placed on top of the plywood will prevent animals from pushing the plywood off and escaping.

- *Pitfall trap:* A pitfall trap can be formed easily when an empty, 2 lb. coffee can is buried upright in the ground with its top edge level with the soil along a small animal trail. Animals running along the trail will fall into the can and be unable to jump back out to freedom.

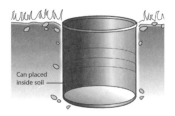

Can placed inside soil

Activity 69. Observing Decomposition (preK–8)

NSES Science Content Standards

- Unifying concepts and processes in science
- Science as inquiry
- Life science

Additional materials: jar or can with lid

What happens to animals and plants after they die? Careful observation of dead animals or plants on the school grounds will answer this question. Locate a small dead animal in the schoolyard. So that other animals do not disturb the process, place the dead animal on soil in a jar or can and screw on a lid with plenty of holes in its top. Leave the dead animal in the container outside but routinely observe it over the course of a week. Have students draw pictures and write in their nature journals what they see in the jar or can (on the sides of the container as well as on the animal). Note the number of days it takes for the animal to nearly disappear and which parts take the longest to decompose. This activity can also be done with dead plants. Just establish a pile of dead vegetation in an unused area of the schoolyard, and observe how it changes and disappears. *Students must wear gloves when handling dead animals.*

Activity 70. Dissecting Animals (4–8)

NSES Science Content Standards

- Unifying concepts and processes in science
- Science as inquiry
- Life science

Note: Teachers should consider sending permission notes home with students for this activity, as some parents and/or students may be opposed to dissection.

Dead animals found in a schoolyard can be carefully dissected by students. Specialized dissection equipment is not necessary for this activity; a pair of scissors, wooden pencils, a magnifying glass, and tweezers are the only materials necessary. However, you must constantly supervise the animal dissection, and students must wear aprons, gloves, and protective eyewear while dissecting. It is important that in their vigor to investigate the animal, students do not jump into the dissection without care. Break the dissection down into small sections and ask students to look for specific items. For example, ask students to carefully isolate 10 different structures in an animal, place each item on a sheet of paper without breaking it, then identify each of the items. A more difficult challenge is to list 10 different structures whose functions students know. Remains of dissected animals should be disposed of by incineration.

a. Dissecting vertebrate animals: mammals and birds (4–8)

Because of anatomical similarities with humans, animals that contain bones are always interesting for students to take apart. To discourage decay and micro-organism growth, the animal selected for dissection should have died recently. Wearing protective goggles and clothing, students should carefully remove or cut away many of the external features, such as skin and hair. Make the first incision through the chest and abdomen from the belly side of the animal with a strong pair of scissors. This will expose the organs of the chest and abdominal cavities. Check reference books to help identify the organs. Students may also find the forceps and long straight pins useful in the dissection to help hold things as they work through the dissection.

b. Dissecting vertebrate animals: reptiles, amphibians, and fish (4–8)

Vertebrates that do not possess hair or feathers are relatively easy to prepare. Again, students should wear aprons, gloves, and protective goggles. To avoid disease and unpleasant odors, dissections of vertebrates should be performed only on animals that have died recently. Anatomical features on the lower vertebrates are sometimes different enough to discourage novice investigators. Consequently, you should have pertinent dissection manuals handy for accurate identification, along with scissors, forceps, and straight pins.

c. Dissecting invertebrate animals: arthropods, mollusks, and worms (4–8)

As a point of comparison, boneless animals present an interesting dilemma to students who want to dissect. There are no support structures under the skin to support or hook things. Some invertebrates, such as grasshoppers, have a flexible, external shell called an *exoskeleton*, which provides attachment points for muscles and other organs, while other invertebrates, such as earthworms, rely on their muscles to provide shape and protect their organs. Pairs of sharp scissors, forceps, and long straight pins are the dissecting tools for all invertebrates. Again, participants should wear aprons, gloves, and protective goggles when dissecting.

Topic: Vertebrates and
Invertebrates
Go to: *www.scilinks.org*
Code: SYS028

Activity 71. Incubating a Bird or Reptile Egg (preK–8)

NSES Science Content Standards

- Unifying concepts and processes in science
- Science as inquiry
- Life science
- Science in personal and social perspectives

Additional materials: wide-mouth jar (pickle or other glass jar) (71a,b,c); compost or leaf litter (71a); plastic wrap (71a); cotton balls (71b); nonmercury Fahrenheit thermometer (71c)

Periodically a student will find an unhatched bird or reptile egg on school grounds. This provides an excellent opportunity for the class to observe the inner portion of an egg and a developing embryo. First, there is one major difference between a bird and a reptile egg: Bird eggs are enclosed in a hard shell, while reptile eggs are enclosed in a leathery, pliable shell. Both types of shells have tiny pores through which gases diffuse in or out of the egg, and both types of eggs contain a nutrient-rich yolk, amniotic fluid, and a support liquid in which the embryo rests. Reptile eggs are often found in leaf piles or soft soil around the grounds, while bird eggs are generally found in tall grass in an unplowed field or on the lawn below a nest.

a. If a reptile egg is found (4–8)

Students should find a wide-mouth jar (pickle or other glass jars work well) and fill half the jar with coarse compost or leaf litter. Do not remove the fungus-eating bugs or round worms in the compost. Students should make a depression with their thumb for each of the eggs to rest in so that the eggs do not touch. Class members can mist water on the egg and compost until the liquid begins to appear on the bottom of the jar, then cover the container with a piece of plastic wrap secured by a rubber band. The students should poke a small hole or two in the wrap and set the incubator in a warm spot but not in direct sunlight. After about six weeks, the egg's shell will begin to collapse inward, which should alert the investigator the egg will hatch shortly.

b. If a hard-shelled bird egg is found: embryo or not (4–8)

The same wide-mouth jar can be used for a bird egg, but cotton is placed in the jar rather than compost. In many states, it is illegal to incubate eggs of wild birds, so students should check with the local extension office or wildlife management organization. The safest way to raise eggs through hatching is to purchase a few fertile eggs from a farmer. It will not be possible to guarantee the eggs will hatch because fertility of eggs cannot be determined before incubating them for a brief time. After about three days, students can hold an egg in front of a candle or light to expose the shadow of a developing embryo. The candling method can also be used to see if a bird egg found on the school grounds contains an embryo or not.

c. Incubating a bird egg (preK–8)

If a bird egg is to be incubated, it should be placed on cotton in the wide-mouth jar with its larger, more rounded end slightly higher than its smaller, more pointed end (a larger incubator should be constructed for larger eggs). A small, nonmercury Fahrenheit ther-mometer should be placed in the jar with the egg to allow the temperature of the incuba-tor to be maintained near 98°F and a light mist should be sprayed on the egg and cotton once or twice a day. Bird eggs also need to be turned once or twice a day, so the misting and turning can be done at the same time (do not turn bird eggs a day or two before hatching). Changes in the shape of the egg or the appearance of tiny holes or cracks will signal that the egg will hatch soon. After the egg has hatched, allow the young bird to remain in the incubator for at least 24 hours. Initially, the new hatchling will not be hungry because birds ingest the remaining egg yolk before hatching to obtain their initial nutrition.

d. Caring for a baby bird or injured bird (preK–8)

If a baby bird is found on the school grounds and clearly has fallen from a nest, students should place it back in the nest. If the nest is no longer in one piece, students should place scraps of the nest and the baby bird in a small box and secure it where the original nest once was. Many times the parents will return and continue to feed the baby. There is an unfounded belief that handling a baby or injured bird will leave a human smell on the bird that will cause the parents to abandon it. This is untrue because birds tend to have an extremely poor sense of smell. It is true, however, that taking the bird home as a pet is illegal, unless a person is licensed as a wildlife rehabilitator.

Activity 72. Fish and Amphibians (preK–8)

NSES Science Content Standards
- Unifying concepts and processes in science
- Science as inquiry
- Life science

Raising fish and amphibians may be one of the easiest projects to do in a schoolyard setting. Fish and amphibians are very hardy and tend to develop and hatch quickly, especially those found in seasonal ponds or wet areas. In addition to the fun of watching the organisms develop, students can compare different types of organisms and their special adaptations.

a. Rearing frog, salamander, or fish eggs (preK–8)

Frogs, salamanders, and fish lay hundreds of gelatinous eggs in the early spring each year. When students discover them, either on a nature walk in the area or in ponds, streams, and puddles at home, they will notice tiny embryos wriggling within the jelly mass. They will need to scoop up several dozen eggs and, if a pond is not available, place them in a children's pool or aquarium in the schoolyard. Students observe them daily, keeping a record of their growth in a field report. Students should add some algae from the pond or stream the egg mass was found in so the young hatchlings can eat and grow. If students cannot find enough algae, they can add washed boiled lettuce or strained spinach that can be purchased from a market as baby food. The embryos of frogs, salamanders, and fish will grow quickly, and before long, they will transform into tiny adults. At this stage, students will need to lower the water level quite a bit and place a small log or rock in the center of the pool so the young organisms can

SCI LINKS
THE WORLD'S A CLICK AWAY

Topic: Amphibians
Go to: *www.scilinks.org*
Code: SYS029

Topic: Fishes
Go to: *www.scilinks.org*
Code: SYS030

climb out of the water. In a schoolyard pond, the organisms can generally climb out of the water at the edges. To encourage fruit flies to come to the rock or log, students can place a banana peel or two on the "island." Fruit flies are a delectable food for the young frogs, salamanders, and fish.

b. Comparing frogs and toads (preK–8)

Young students sometimes have difficulty distinguishing the difference between a frog and a toad. The differences become obvious, however, when the two amphibians are compared side by side. Despite the structural similarities, frogs have moist, slimy, thin skin, and toads have leathery, thick skin. Both frogs and toads are readily found in a schoolyard area rich with vegetation and moisture, such as around a pool or pond. Student teams can research the difference between toads and frogs in the library or on the internet before heading outdoors and can assist with the teacher's explanations once both are found.

Activity 73. Examining Skeletons (preK–8)

NSES Science Content Standards
* Unifying concepts and processes in science
* Science as inquiry
* Life science

Additional materials: forceps, magnifying glasses

Students sometimes enjoy reassembling an animal that has been dissected more than they like disassembling it. This is particularly true with the skeleton of various vertebrates. To remove the excess tissue from the bones of a recently dissected animal, the bony skeleton should be left outside in an unobtrusive area of the school grounds for several weeks. Then submerge the skeleton in a strong bleach solution for another two to three weeks. Dry the bones outdoors for another week. When the bones are finally prepared, the teacher should make sure the bones are taken apart before presenting the skeleton to participants. Students can lay the bones on a flat board and glue them in place, or the bones can be wired together to create a three-dimensional model.

a. Examining the inside of a bone (preK–8)

Students are usually surprised to learn that bones are composed of living cells and, as such, they grow, bleed, and experience pain. Bones are hard because their cells absorb minerals, primarily calcium. Under the mineral mantle, bones are riddled with support fibers and, in the long bones, hollow shafts. While the cells of a preserved skeleton are no longer alive, the large holes in bone and the support fibers that allowed the passage of blood vessels and nerve fibers are easy to find. The entrance holes for the nerves and vessels are usually near the ends of the bony, knucklelike ends of the bone. The fibrous internal structures and central canals can best be seen by sawing the bone completely through at its end using an appropriate tool such as a saw or serrated knife, depending on the size of the bone, and through the middle of its central shaft.

b. Comparing different animal bones (preK–8)

Students are sometimes surprised to find that a skeleton is composed of many bones. There are long bones and short bones, round bones and flat bones, and bones that do not seem to fit any description. This sets up the opportunity for students to compare various bones of a skeleton that was found in the schoolyard. Students also can compare features of the bones and predict the function of each feature.

c. Differences between joint types in a skeleton (preK–8)

As students assemble a skeleton, they will quickly observe differences in the locations where bones come together. These junctions are better known as *joints*, and students will immediately notice three different joint types as they put the skeleton together. Perhaps the most obvious is the *ball-and-socket joint* at the hip and shoulder, in which a smooth end of one bone fits nicely into a pocket of another bone or two. Students should notice the great range of motion this joint provides by watching a team-mate maneuver his or her shoulder or leg. A second joint students notice on the skeleton occurs at the elbow, knee, and fingers. Students will see immediately as they move their analogous joint that this junction works like a hinge, allowing movement on a single plane. This action gives the junction its name, *hinge joint*. The third joint most easily recognized is the rockerlike joint at the neck that allows the skull to rock forward and backward and side to side. This joint is called a *pivot joint*. Students will see that there are junctions that do not fit any of the above descriptions. There are *gliding joints* between the vertebrae, *sliding joints* at the wrist and ankles, and *saddle joints* at the base of the thumb. There are also *immovable joints* within the skull and in the hip girdle.

d. Dissecting owl pellets (preK–8)

This activity has become popular with classes because it is now possible to purchase owl pellets from commercial vendors. However, teachers do not have to purchase owl pellets because they are easily found in nature, especially near an old barn, shed, or oak tree. Owl pellets are small packets of bones, teeth, feathers, hair, and other indigestible body parts of prey regurgitated by owls several hours after they have eaten. Because the pellets have come from the inside of a wild animal, they may contain bacteria and other micro-organisms; therefore, students should be careful when collecting them. Students should always wear gloves, goggles, and facial masks, and place the pellets in a bucket rather than a field bag. In the schoolyard at a table set up with a hot plate, students (still wear-ing rubber gloves) should wrap each pellet in a gauze bag and tie it tightly at its neck. The gauze bag should be marked with the team's name and placed in a pot on the cool

hot plate. When all the bags are tied, a 3–5% solution of sodium hydroxide should be poured over the bagged pellets and the liquid heated to near boiling. This action kills any microbes in the pellet that may cause problems. After about five minutes, students (using gloves) should remove and open their bags. The boiling should also have cleanly separated the hair and feathers from the hard parts in the pellet and the bones, and teeth can be extracted with forceps and examined with a magnifying glass. As with any dissection, students should wash their hands thoroughly after the exercise. *An alternative method to prepare owl pellets is to heat them in an oven at 170° F for 24 hours. This also kills the associated microbial parasites. Students again should be reminded to wear rubber gloves, safety goggles, and masks when dissecting owl pellets found in the wild.*

Activity 74. Studying Fish Anatomy (preK–8)

NSES Science Content Standards
- Unifying concepts and processes in science
- Science as inquiry
- Life science

Fish are easy vertebrates to study and are fairly easy to obtain. Most students are aware of fish but have never truly observed them. For example, students do not know how many fins fish commonly have. Challenge students to draw a fish from memory, paying particular attention to the number and placement of its fins. While naming the fins should not be required in this challenge, you may want to ask students to label the names of the various types of fins on their drawing (*dorsal, caudal, anal, pelvic,* and *pectoral*). Have students compare their drawings to live fish once they have finished; they will often be surprised at the differences!

a. Fin functions (preK–8)

Knowing where the fins are is important in determining what each fin does. Students can determine a fin's function by watching a small group of fish swimming in a large aquarium, shallow pond, or children's pool in the schoolyard. Allow student teams several minutes to watch several fish swimming. Students can carefully stick a small twig into the water to encourage the fish to veer sharply left or right to note the action of various fins. Note how the fins behave when the fish dives to deeper levels and rises to the surface. The challenge in this exercise is to come up with at least one function for each type of fin.

b. Fish dissection (4–8)

Note: Depending on your school's policies, you may want to send a permission note home with students before doing this activity.

Most parents have seen the inside of a fish, but many students have not. In this exercise, students cut open a freshly killed fish, using a knife, scissors, or other appropriate tools to expose the inner body cavity. Challenge students to identify the various body organs in the fish before they check out a diagram in a resource book. Students should try to correctly identify five different structures.

Activity 75. Studying Squirrels (preK–8)

NSES Science Content Standards

- Unifying concepts and processes in science
- Science as inquiry
- Life science

This activity can be done with either ground squirrels (chipmunks) or tree squirrels (gray squirrels) most of the year; ground squirrels hibernate during the coldest months while tree squirrels do not hibernate and are often seen in winter. Squirrels are generally not hard to find as they industriously scurry about tending to their needs. Challenge students to observe one or more squirrels in the schoolyard for several minutes and come up with five behaviors that seem unique to them (e.g., Do they use their tails for balance?).

a. Discovering tree squirrel nesting sites (preK–8)

Gray squirrels live in the cavities of trees that they frequently enlarge and pad with fallen leaves, or they construct large, leafy nests wedged firmly between forked branches high in trees. These nests are always built in a tree that stands near other trees to ensure escape routes via neighboring branches, and they have only one opening for entry and exit. Ground squirrels, on the other hand, use burrows in the ground that have several entrances and escape openings. If they cannot find an existing burrow, they will dig channels into the ground, removing the soil using the side pouches of their mouths. When they reach the surface, chipmunks will spit the soil randomly around the area to make the burrow opening less obvious. Challenge teams to find three tree squirrel nests and three ground squirrel burrows around the school grounds.

b. Discovering food preferences of squirrels (preK–8)

Squirrels constantly look for food, whether they are hungry or not. When they find food, they usually sit and immediately begin to eat it, holding the food in their front paws. Food storage is an instinctive drive of squirrels, and stockpiling is found in every species of these rodents. Many different things are eaten by ground and tree squirrels. Careful observation of the squirrels' behavior on the school grounds should reveal some of their preferred foods. Teams should try to come up with at least five different foods eaten by either tree or ground squirrels.

> Squirrels usually feed on nuts, plant buds, fruits, and berries, but they will occasionally devour insects and small frogs and sometimes even take eggs or young birds from their nest.

c. Discovering hoarding sites of squirrels (preK–8)

Tree squirrels often hoard food in the hollows of trees, under wood and rock piles, and underground; ground squirrels will also bury seeds, but most seeds are stored inside rooms in their burrows. One common belief is that squirrels quickly forget where they have buried their food, which assists in the replanting of vegetation. However, a recent study has found that as young plants sprout through the soil, the squirrels are reminded of their planting and devour the seedlings. With careful observation, students can discover signs of squirrels' burying on the school grounds. See if each team can find three squirrel stashes.

d. Reproductive behavior of squirrels (preK–8)

> Courting adult squirrels playfully chase, snuggle, and groom each other, while youngsters chase, wrestle, and playfully nip others' ears, necks, and legs.

Squirrels mate in midwinter, and females give birth with the onset of spring. If the food supplies are abundant, squirrels will again mate in early summer and have another litter in early autumn. A month after young squirrels are born, they begin to move around on their own in the nest. Adult squirrel behavior before mating and young squirrel behavior upon leaving the nest are very different than the squirrel behaviors observed in a previous exercise. Teams should see if they can discern three different behaviors of active squirrels in the schoolyard.

Activity 76. Studying Birds (preK–8)

NSES Science Content Standards

- Unifying concepts and processes in science
- Science as inquiry
- Life science
- Science in personal and social perspectives
- History and nature of science

Bird watching is the most popular hobby in the nation, and usually some students in the class have experienced it with their parents. This generally involves identifying a bird through its songs and appearance, then recording the bird in a field book.

a. Spotting different kinds of birds (preK–8)

Topic: Bird
    Characteristics
Go to: *www.scilinks.org*
Code: SYS032

While knowing birds by songs or names is laudable, it is difficult for students to initially get excited about it. A good way to get students started is to have them look for different kinds of birds without worrying about names. Challenge students to locate 10 different kinds of birds on the school grounds within a specific time limit (e.g., 20 minutes). They can write a brief description of each bird they see to explain how they were able to tell the different kinds apart.

b. Finding different kinds of bird nests (preK–8)

Students and teachers are often surprised by the number of bird nests that can be found around a large schoolyard. A scan through the tree foliage will likely reveal two or three different kinds of nests, and some can be discovered under porches or along fences. Several bird species make their nests in thick shrubbery, while other species nest on the ground. Challenge student teams to come up with five different nest sites on the schoolyard, being careful not to disturb the nests. In many areas, it is illegal to take or possess nests from wild birds without a special permit.

Topic: Kind of Birds
Go to: *www.scilinks.org*
Code: SYS033

c. Finding different kinds of bird feathers (preK–8)

A great way to develop interest in birds is to have student teams look for and identify different bird feathers. This can be difficult, so do not make it too rigorous. Challenge students to find three different kinds of feathers around the schoolyard and identify the type of bird the feathers came from in a specific period of time. Check local regulations regarding the collection of wild bird feathers.

d. Finding different colors of birds (preK–3)

Another easy way to develop interest in birds is to have students look for birds of different colors. Most birds are two or more colors; however, students can count a bird that is mostly a single color (e.g., blue jays). Challenge students to find 10 different-color birds around the school.

This activity will be fun for all students, but young children will find it particularly interesting. A few birds with distinct color displays include blue (blue jays, bluebirds, indigo buntings), red (cardinals, scarlet tanagers), yellow (yellow warbler, goldfinch), green (red-eyed vireo, ruby-throated hummingbird), orange (Baltimore orioles, black-headed grosbeaks), black (crows, blackbirds), gray (juncos, titmouse, gnatcatchers), and brown (waxwings, thrashers, sparrows).

e. Finding different ways birds get around on the ground (preK–8)

Students can focus on a specific type of behavior after they have had a chance to observe different birds that come to the schoolyard. Challenge students to find five different ways that birds move on the ground.

Students will quickly observe that birds have different preferences for moving around on the ground. Some birds will walk from place to place (crows, pigeons), some birds will hop (house finches), some will run (killdeer), and some will land, then fly to the next spot (hummingbird). And some birds do not land on the ground or a plant from the time they leave the nest in the morning until the time they return at night (chimney swift).

f. Finding different types of feet on birds (preK–8)

Students can also observe the feet of birds found in a schoolyard; they are often surprised at the varieties that exist. Challenge teams to come up with five different patterns or types of bird feet.

Students will quickly notice two or three types of birds' feet: three toes forward, one back (robins), webbed toe walkers/swimmers (ducks), two toes forward and two back (woodpeckers). Not seen as often are the tiny-toed feet of chimney swifts and hummingbirds, or the sharp talons of hawks, eagles, and owls.

g. Finding different types of beaks on birds (preK–8)

Many students do not realize that the beaks of birds are not all the same, but with careful observation (and perhaps magnification with binoculars) they quickly realize that there is a vast difference. The challenge in this exercise is to find three different types of beaks on the birds that visit the schoolyard.

Students are often surprised by how easily this is accomplished with careful searching. For example, they will find that sparrows have short, stubby beaks for cracking seed, and starlings have long, narrow beaks for catching insects in holes. Woodpeckers also have long beaks, but they are thicker and wider than starlings. Hummingbirds have long, strawlike beaks to draw nectar, and hawks have strong, wide beaks that are generally hooked at the end.

h. Imitating a bird (preK–3)

Topic: Bird Adaptations
Go to: *www.scilinks.org*
Code: SYS034

This activity is especially fun for younger students because they love to imitate animals. Students decide what bird they want to be and look in reference books to find more about the bird's behaviors, songs or calls, and diet. When the student imitates his or her particular bird, the other students should be given a chance to identify which bird the presenter is imitating.

9 Experimenting With How Animals Work

Activity 77. Comparing Jumping Ability in Insects (preK–8)

NSES Science Content Standards

- Unifying concepts and processes in science
- Science as inquiry
- Life science

Additional materials: clear glass or plastic containers

Topic: Insects
Go to: *www.scilinks.org*
Code: SYS023

Jumping organisms have always held a fascination for children. Holding competitions with different kinds or sizes of jumping insects can be a fun way to look at body length and jumping distance comparisons.

Students can capture several crickets and grasshoppers and place them in clear glass or plastic containers for observation. Challenge students to identify at least four similarities and four differences. Let them identify the various cricket and grasshopper species they caught. Most people do not realize that there are many different kinds of these insects found in most areas around a school. Students can predict which ones will jump farthest based on their observations.

When they have completed their observations, it is time for a contest! Have each group choose one or two insects that they will handle for the contest. Students measure the body length of their grasshoppers and crickets, so they can later compare which ones jumped farthest based on the size of the insect. Prepare an open area on the school grounds where the insects can jump without landing on a tree, plant, or building, so students can get accurate measurements of at least three jumps for each insect. If a large open area is not available, the groups will need to take turns to avoid insect paths crossing and causing confusion. Students should have a net handy to recapture the insects, but some will probably escape after their jump. One student is the handler for each insect, placing it at the starting point, marked with an *X*. Another student from each group is the marker, marking each jump the insect makes with chalk or a small rock. Students then measure and record the distance between each point.

Once the contest is over, the insects can be released. Groups can then average the numbers for their insects and calculate how many times their body length they were able to jump. Which ones jumped the greatest distance? Which insects jumped the greatest number of body lengths? Students can graph their results for comparison and can write about the different insects they caught in their nature journals.

Activity 78. Exploring Jumping in Frogs (preK–8)

NSES Science Content Standards

- Unifying concepts and processes in science
- Science as inquiry
- Life science

A frog jumping contest demonstrates the similarities and differences in another jumping organism. As with the grasshoppers and crickets previously discussed, you can find several frog species in the United States. If possible, let the students catch their own frogs during a field trip or at a pond or wetland area on the school grounds; hold the contest nearby so frogs can be easily returned to their habitat. If this is not an option, the teacher, some students, or a nearby nature center may be able to collect enough frogs for the activity. Bullfrogs are favorites for jumping contests because of their large size, but students can do the body length and jumping distance comparison to see if they really jump farther than other frog species. Students can place their frogs at a marked location, or they can all start at a line and see which one jumps farthest. Use a meterstick to measure how far each frog can jump in a single leap, and record the results for all frogs. Students should not lose their frogs! Once the contest has ended and the frogs are returned safely to their habitat, students can graph the results.

SC**LINKS**.
THE WORLD'S A CLICK AWAY
Topic: Frogs
Go to: *www.scilinks.org*
Code: SYS035

Activity 79. Exploring the Strength of Insects (preK–8)

NSES Science Content Standards
- Unifying concepts and processes in science
- Science as inquiry
- Physical science
- Life science
- Science and technology

Additional materials: petri dish or other lightweight, shallow plastic container

Another way to compare organisms is to observe how strong they are. Many types of insects can carry or pull several times their own weight, and students will have fun catching the insects and comparing their strength.

a. Beetle pulling contest (4–8)

Students can design a fascinating demonstration of the strength of bess beetles, which are easily located in oak trees around a school during fall. Bess beetles live in colonies in decaying stumps and logs. They prefer hardwood such as oak, elm, and other deciduous trees, especially when the wood is well decayed and falls apart easily.

Once students have collected some beetles, they can devise a harness using dental floss or other fine string. Attach one end to the beetle and the other end to a plastic petri dish or other lightweight, shallow plastic container. The lid from a clear plastic deli container also works well. Place pennies or washers in the dish, one at a time, to see how many pennies the beetles can pull. Hold the contest on a rough surface such as a sidewalk or playground so that the beetles can develop enough traction to get moving.

Student groups can measure the speed, weight pulled (make sure you include the weight of the empty petri dish or plastic lid), and distance traveled. They can also weigh the beetle and compare their body mass to the amount of weight they can pull. Students can calculate how much weight they could pull if they were as strong as their beetles! Older students may also be interested in calculating physics concepts such as the coefficient of friction, work done, and power.

b. Food transportation limits of ants (preK–8)

Ants can be found almost anywhere, even in urban and suburban schoolyards. How many different kinds of ants can students find? Encourage students to observe the ants to see where they go. Place an obstacle in the ants' path and observe what happens. Students can try different-size pebbles or sticks and see if the ants move them, go around them, or climb over them. Does the next ant following that path take the same route around the obstacle, or does it try something new?

Use these amazing insects to demonstrate the remarkable strength of some very small organisms. While ants are too small to weigh on most scales, students can still compare the size of various food items that ants carry. If there is an ant colony in the schoolyard, these ants can be used for this activity. If not, collect some ants for the class to use or build your own ant colony and observe those individuals. Students can start by placing small pieces of different food near the paths ants are taking to and from their colony. Some suggestions might be small seeds, oatmeal, or small pieces of bread. Students can also try different cold cereals. How large a piece can a single ant carry? Students estimate how many times their weight ants can carry. They will find that ants can pull or carry 10–50 times their own weight! The students can calculate how much weight they themselves could carry if they were as strong as an ant.

Activity 80. Comparing the Eyes of Invertebrates and Vertebrates (4–8)

NSES Science Content Standards
- Unifying concepts and processes in science
- Science as inquiry
- Life science

Additional materials: jars or large droppers (e.g., turkey baster), 2 L bottle or other clear plastic container, magnifying glasses

Most students realize what eyes do but not how they differ from one animal to another. In this exercise, students investigate the eyes of three completely different animals: water fleas, houseflies, and frogs.

- *Water fleas:* Water fleas, or *daphnia*, are small crustaceans that inhabit plant-rich, unpolluted ponds in North America. The fleas are quickly harmed by strong pesticides, bleach, and pollutants. They are hardy little bugs with a transparent outer skeleton, making them an ideal animal for studying various body systems. Water fleas are interesting because they have two compound eyes when young that grow together to form one large eye as adults. The eye is easily seen in the head area of the animal near the antennae. This eye sees things as blurry forms and detects gross movements of objects in the environment. Daphnia also have a much smaller simple eye just below the large eye called an *ocellus*. This eye is intertwined in a mass of nerves and is more difficult to locate.

  Daphnia are easily caught with a large dropper pipette, such as a turkey baster, or in a wide-mouth jar. When found, they can be kept in a clean 2 L bottle with the neck cut off or in another clear plastic container, half full of pond water, for several days without damage. Challenge student teams to locate several dozen water fleas and list five features of both the compound and simple eyes.

- *Houseflies:* Unlike the aquatic water fleas, flies are terrestrial and easily located on the school grounds. Houseflies also possess a pair of compound eyes and a simple eye, but their eyes are suited for a dry environment. Careful observation will reveal that the eye is made up of hundreds of tiny lens-covered, pigmented cylinders, each leading to a tiny nerve cell. Each lens in a compound eye is independent of the other, resulting in a mosaic pattern of the image in the brain. The eyes cannot focus, so insects are terribly nearsighted. Honeybees, for example, can see objects best at 8–10 in. away. They are attracted to flowers by scent and motion of the plants. Butterflies, on the other hand, can see best at several feet away; this enables them to see the flowers they will visit as they approach a garden. The simple eye of most insects is located between the two compound eyes and assists with motion detection farther away. These insects can readily be caught in wide-mouth jars in which a small bit of raw meat is placed. Leave the baited jar in a sunny spot on a table on the school grounds for about 30 minutes. Flies will be drawn to the jar by the odor from the warming meat. When students return to the jar, they must quickly place the jar lid on top to trap the flies inside. To settle the flies, the jar should be placed in a cold ice chest for 20–30 minutes; then they can be easily removed and studied with a magnifying glass for about 10 minutes. If the flies begin to quiver, students can put them back on ice for a while. Challenge teams to find five features of the housefly eye to compare with the water flea. *Always wear gloves when handling raw meat. Wash hands thoroughly with soap and water when finished.*

- *Frogs:* The eyes of the frog, a vertebrate, are quite different from the invertebrates seen earlier. Rather than multilens, compound, and simple eyes, frogs' eyes are large, single-lens, spherical structures; they do not have a simple eye. The pigmented eyes bulge from the head, which allows the frog not only to look for

Topic: Vertebrates and Invertebrates

Go to: *www.scilinks.org*

Code: SYS028

prey with most of its body below the water but also to rotate its eyes nearly 180 degrees without turning its head. Interestingly, the two eyes in amphibians are not coordinated in sight, so binocular vision is not possible. The frog does not seem to be greatly disadvantaged by this, however, for it can accurately catch prey midflight without much difficulty: The single lens of the eye can be moved forward or backward to quickly bring prey into focus.

Frogs also have two eyelids that they use to keep their eyes moist while out of water. Students will notice the upper lid is a folded flap of skin, which differs from the more membranous lower lid. This bottom lid, called the *nictitating membrane*, covers the eye under water. The upper membrane is used to completely darken the eye when the frog is resting or when it swallows. Student teams should try to predict why frogs must close their eyes tightly when they swallow.

These amphibians can generally be caught more easily on land than in water. When frogs are in a pond, students will likely have to use a long-handled net to catch them. Once they are caught, students should wrap the frog in a wet cloth or several layers of damp paper towels and secure the wrapping with two or three rubber bands, making sure they are not too tight. Once the frog is calm, its eyes can be examined with a magnifier. Challenge teams to locate five distinct features of the frog eye to compare with the eyes of invertebrates.

> Frogs cannot use their tongues or jaws to swallow. The frog therefore pulls its eyes, forcefully into the eye socket, which depresses them into the mouth cavity. This action forces food backward into the throat and initiates the swallowing contractions of the throat muscles.

Activity 81. Fish Behavior (4–8)

NSES Science Content Standards

- Unifying concepts and processes in science
- Science as inquiry
- Life science

After examining the anatomy of fish in earlier activities, students can use the fish to study the physiological effects of activity and temperature. In addition, other behaviors can be examined easily in fish. These activities familiarize students with observing and recording experimental data.

a. Respiration rate and stress relationships (4–8)

Most students realize that when they are being chased in a game of tag, their breathing rate increases. Does this also happen when animals less complex than humans are chased? Teams should discuss this question and come up with a hypothesis. Challenge students to figure out a way to determine the respiration rate of fish, then set up an experiment on the school grounds to test this hypothesis.

b. Respiration rate and temperature fluctuation relationships (4–8)

The internal temperatures of fish change with the external environment, so they represent nicely how cold-blooded animals respond to external events. When the water temperature goes down, the body systems in the fish slow down; when the water temperature goes up, the metabolism also increases. Challenge teams to come up with a way to measure the rate at which fish breathe in 60 seconds at different water temperatures. So the fish is not harmed, students should not change the water temperature more than 10 degrees above or below the original environmental temperature.

c. Can fish be taught? (4–8)

Students are often curious to see if animals can be taught to do something. Studies have found most animals can learn simple, recurring behaviors. For example, fish in a pond can learn to swim to a particular region along the shore to be fed, and fish will spend more time in a pool painted a soothing color (e.g., light blue) than a harsher color (e.g., bright red). Challenge teams to design their own experiment in a schoolyard pond or nearby area to determine whether fish in a natural environment can be taught a particular behavior.

SCILINKS.
THE WORLD'S A CLICK AWAY

Topic: Fish
Go to: www.scilinks.org
Code: SYS036

d. Do fish prefer to swim in schools or alone? (4–8)

In this fun activity, the outcome depends on the type of fish students are investigating. Many ocean fish seek protection in numbers, while freshwater fish often tend to prefer fewer neighbors. Challenge students to investigate the schooling behaviors of the fish in the school pond or children's pool. Teams form a hypothesis that they can investigate in a controlled setting.

> A good way to do this exploration is to isolate different-size populations of the same species of fish in large, clear containers (such as gallon pickle jars) in the larger pool or tub and see how the rest of the population of that fish species responds to various-size groups.

Activity 82. Fish Buoyancy (4–8)

NSES Science Content Standards

- Unifying concepts and processes in science
- Science as inquiry
- Physical science
- Life science
- Science and technology

Students may wonder how a fish maintains its depth (buoyancy) in the water. The answer lies with a horizontal, balloonlike bladder just under the backbone of the fish. Fish can increase the amount of air in the bladder by drawing gas into or out of their blood and into or out of the air bladder. A fun investigation of buoyancy can be done with balloons

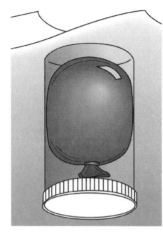

and small, different-size, cylindrical glass or plastic containers. Bottles for pills, vitamins, spices, or jellies work well. To make a buoyancy tester, put a deflated balloon in a bottle and inflate it. Knot the balloon and hold it in the bottle with a rubber band. If the buoyancy tester is small, more rubber bands can be added to make it sink. Teams will realize that the more rubber bands they add, the deeper in the water the tester will sink. Alternatively, students can use the same size and weight for their buoyancy testers and can instead inflate balloons with different volumes of air. As teams investigate this process, they should attempt to determine which method applies to fish.

Activity 83. Studying Circulation in the Webbing of Frog Feet (4–8)

NSES Science Content Standards
- Unifying concepts and processes in science
- Science as inquiry
- Life science
- Earth and space science

Like mammals, amphibians have vessels to carry blood to and from the heart. Blood circulation in the thin skin between a frog's toes is easily observed with a magnifying glass. Students should carefully wrap a captured frog in a wet paper towel and hold it marginally tight with a rubber band. As students place their frogs on a table in bright sunlight, a partner should carefully pull its leg down away from the body and gently spread out the webbing between the toes. When this is done, another teammate can observe the blood flowing in the foot using a magnifying glass. When the team members notice the pulsations of the blood in the vessel, they should count the number of pulsations per minute. This will give students a record of the heartbeats per minute. Record this number and compare it with the beats per minute obtained by other teams. This activity can also be done with the caudal fin of fish. *Wash hands thoroughly with soap and water when finished.*

Activity 84. Altering the Breathing Rate of a Frog (4–8)

NSES Science Content Standards

- Unifying concepts and processes in science
- Science as inquiry
- Life science

Students are fascinated by experimenting (humanely) with animals. An easy experiment that can be done with frogs investigates the effect of temperature on respiration rate. Students observe that the throat of a frog at rest moves up and down. This action decreases pressure in the frog's throat, causing air to rush into its lungs. Students also notice that the temperature of its surroundings has an effect on a frog's breathing rate. Challenge teams to come up with an experiment that answers this question: How does temperature fluctuation in the schoolyard environment affect the frog's breathing rate? You may want students to graph the results of their study.

10 Exploring Energy

Activity 85. Wing Shapes and Aerodynamics in Birds (preK–8)

NSES Science Content Standards

- Unifying concepts and processes in science
- Science as inquiry
- Physical science
- Life science
- Earth and space science
- Science and technology

Topic: Classification of Birds
Go to: *www.scilinks.org*
Code: SYS037

In this fun learning experiment, student teams research different bird species, noting where the birds live and how they feed and protect themselves, and examining the different shapes of their wings. Once students have studied several species, challenge the teams to create their own birds modeled after one of the species they studied. They can create their model using construction paper, or they may prefer lightweight cardboard cut into a body shape with a slit for the wings to slide through. When they have completed construction of their bird, students can experiment with their models to identify which ones fly farthest, gain the most altitude, or stay aloft longest in an open section of the school grounds. After students have mastered the basics, let them design their own unique bird. Students can experiment with different wing and body features to determine which ones would be most efficient for the needs of the bird they created. Once they have found a design they feel works well, teams can explain to classmates why they chose that particular combination of features.

Activity 86. Heat Absorption in Various Natural Materials (preK–8)

NSES Science Content Standards

- Unifying concepts and processes in science
- Science as inquiry
- Life science
- Earth and space science
- Science and technology
- Science in personal and social perspectives

Students are usually aware that different surfaces get hotter than others, learning, for example, to choose grass over blacktop when walking barefoot. They may not notice that the different colors found in natural materials can make a difference in the amount of heat absorbed.

While studying solar energy, students can look at various ways to collect and store heat from the Sun. Challenge teams to predict what type of material might heat up fastest or store heat the longest, then create an experiment to test their predictions. For this experiment, containers such as tin cans filled with various natural materials will work best. Sand, soil, pebbles, gravel, water, wood shavings, or leaf litter are some examples, but students may also come up with additional ideas. The students will need nonmercury thermometers and a dark-colored box in which to place their containers. Students can arrange their boxes in sunny spots around the school grounds, stirring the contents at 10-min. intervals. Teams should record the temperature of each container every time they stir the contents, for a total of 60 min. Once they have completed the heating portion of this activity, teams can move their boxes to a shady area, monitoring the temperature changes as their materials cool down. Teams can then compare their results to see which materials heated up quickly and which ones retained heat best. Extend the activity by challenging students to look at the areas where these materials were found around the schoolyard and determine how this might affect the plants and animals found there.

SC*LINKS*
THE WORLD'S A CLICK AWAY
Topic: Solar Energy
Go to: *www.scilinks.org*
Code: SYS038

Activity 87. Comparing Heat Reflection With Various Natural Materials (4–8)

NSES Science Content Standards

- Unifying concepts and processes in science
- Science as inquiry
- Life science
- Earth and space science
- Science and technology

Students look at the reflective properties of natural materials to ascertain how this affects plants and wildlife. Challenge students to come up with an activity to determine whether heat reflects differently from various natural surfaces. If the students have difficulty with this challenge, introduce the idea of placing several cups of water in a sunny location in the schoolyard and covering each one with a different material. Ideas students may suggest include green leaves, dead leaves, or bark in various colors, depending on the materials available in the schoolyard. One cup should remain uncovered to compare the reflective properties of water alone and to serve as a control. As students record the temperatures of the cups at regular intervals, they will see which materials heat up fastest and which stay cool longer. By comparing adaptations of features such as skin, coloration, and behavior observed in the different organisms that reside in areas where the natural materials were found, students can look at the effects of heating and cooling properties on living things.

SC*LINKS*
THE WORLD'S A CLICK AWAY
Topic: Heat Energy
Go to: *www.scilinks.org*
Code: SYS039

Activity 88. Make a Solar Oven (4–8)

NSES Science Content Standards

- Unifying concepts and processes in science
- Science as inquiry
- Physical science
- Life science
- Earth and space science
- Science and technology
- Science in personal and social perspectives

Additional materials: cardboard boxes (e.g., pizza box, shoe box), foil

Solar energy is one of the easiest resources for students to harness in useful ways. Solar ovens are very easy to build using common and inexpensive materials. Several designs can be found online, but one of the simplest uses a recycled pizza box. Students carefully cut a flap out of the top, leaving 2–3 in. all the way around the lid. Next, the participants fold the flap back and cover the inside of the flap with foil. They then line the bottom with foil and place a piece of black construction paper over the foil on the bottom, fold down the rest of the lid (with the edge and a hole in the center where the flap folds back), and cover the opening with clear plastic. Students should place the food on the black paper inside, close the lid, and adjust the flap so that the Sun is reflecting into the box. The solar oven can be used to cook foods such as s'mores, hot dogs, or even muffins. An ordinary oven thermometer can be used measure the temperature inside the oven. Food will take longer to cook in the solar oven, and the oven will work better if it is preheated in a sunny spot on the school grounds before the food goes inside. Older students might want to design their own solar cookers to see if they can find a way to cook something faster, heat a larger space, or raise the temperature inside the oven to a certain point the fastest.

Topic: Solar Heated
   Homes
Go to: www.scilinks.org
Code: SYS040

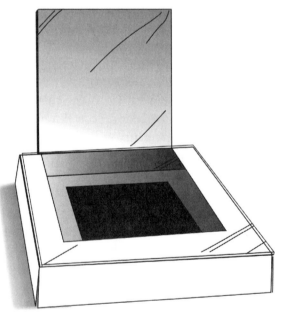

Activity 89. A Water Cycle Model (preK–8)

NSES Science Content Standards
- Unifying concepts and processes in science
- Science as inquiry
- Life science
- Earth and space science
- Science and technology
- Science in personal and social perspectives

Additional materials: glass jars, gravel or pebbles, pie tin or small metal dish, ice cubes

Topic: Water Cycle
Go to: *www.scilinks.org*
Code: SYS041

Water is an essential resource that is necessary for the survival of all organisms. The water cycle (also known as the hydrological cycle) shows how water is recycled through our environment and is a great base to introduce many geological and biological concepts. Knowledge of the water cycle will help students understand how the environment works and how they affect the water cycle every day of their lives.

This interesting activity illustrates the principles of conditions that produce rain. Students can observe the water cycle right in the schoolyard. For this activity, each team should have a glass canning jar; enough gravel or pebbles to have approximately 2 in. at the bottom; and a small pie tin, foil tart pan, or small metal dish that will cover the mouth of the jar completely. Teams will also need access to ice. Provide enough very hot water (120°F) to fill each jar to the top of the gravel. Once the hot water is poured into the jar, students should place the tins over the top and add ice cubes. Students will immediately notice clouds and rain forming and falling back into the hot water below. In their field reports or nature journals, students should explain the similarities and differences between their model and the real water cycle. *Safety note: Remind students to use caution when working with very hot water.*

Activity 90. Effects of Acid Rain (preK–8)

NSES Science Content Standards
- Unifying concepts and processes in science
- Science as inquiry
- Life science
- Science in personal and social perspectives

One form of water cycle pollution is acid rain. Pure deionized water has a pH of 7, but the pH of normal rainfall is between 5 and 6 because rain mixes with natural oxides in the air. Acid rain has a pH of 4.3 in parts of the United States and can be as low as 2 in

Topic: Acid Rain
Go to: www.scilinks.org
Code: SYS042

other parts of the world. Many parts of the world use coal, oil, and natural gas when generating electricity, and scientists have found that air pollution from burning these fossil fuels is the major cause of acid rain. The primary pollutants in the air that lead to acid rain are sulfur dioxide and nitrogen oxide, which mix with water to form sulfuric and nitric acid. These acids are transported in the upper winds over long distances, causing acid rain to fall far away from the source of the pollution.

This activity is an excellent demonstration of the effects of acid rain on living things. Each team has a series of the same potted plants. Students place their plants in a safe location on the school grounds where the same sunlight, wind, and other environmental conditions exist. Team members give each plant the same amount of water every few days but should add vinegar in incremental amounts. A control plant should get only water, while a second plant might get 2 drops of vinegar, a third 20 drops of vinegar, and so on. Students observe the plants over the next two weeks, keeping a record of the amount of vinegar and water each plant has received and the condition of each plant in their field report. After about two weeks, students draw conclusions.

Activity 91. Water Flow (preK–8)

NSES Science Content Standards

- Unifying concepts and processes in science
- Science as inquiry
- Earth and space science
- Science in personal and social perspectives

A common natural energy source that many students are familiar with is moving water. Hydroelectric power and dams are familiar examples, but they may not have had the opportunity to explore how water moves through a waterway.

At a small flowing stream on or near the school grounds, student groups can design a method to measure the speed of the water. If they need assistance, give students a hint by dropping a leaf on the surface so they can watch it float past. Once they have determined a method—which should involve some combination of placing an object on the surface, measuring a specific distance, and timing how long it takes for that object to travel that distance—students can use their plan to measure different parts of the stream, seeing how the water speed changes. What features make the water run faster? What makes it slow down? They can record their results and observations in their field reports. *Be sure to take appropriate safety precautions near the water.*

Activity 92. Water Control (preK–8)

NSES Science Content Standards

- Unifying concepts and processes in science
- Science as inquiry
- Physical science
- Life science
- Earth and space science
- Science and technology
- Science in personal and social perspectives
- History and nature of science

Water flow in natural environments is often changed by outside occurrences, including beavers, fallen trees, or human activities such as logging and mining. This activity gives students a chance to see the effects of these events.

Beavers are extremely good—sometimes too good—at building dams using branches and trees. After finding a small running creek or ditch in or near the schoolyard, students can create a temporary dam using twigs, leaves, and small branches. How effective are these materials? How do they manage to put them together before the parts are washed downstream? What changes occur once the water flow is slowed? How long does it take for the water to rise and spill over the top of the dam? Remind students to dismantle their dams when they are done to maintain the water flow.

Activity 93. Exploring Erosion Control (4–8)

NSES Science Content Standards

- Unifying concepts and processes in science
- Science as inquiry
- Life science
- Earth and space science
- Science and technology
- Science in personal and social perspectives
- History and nature of science

SCI**LINKS**
THE WORLD'S A CLICK AWAY
Topic: Water Erosion
Go to: *www.scilinks.org*
Code: SYS043

Additional materials: large pans; assorted natural items such as gravel, pebbles, twigs, and sand

Erosion can occur when wind or water run too quickly over Earth's surface and carry soil away. One way to minimize erosion is to slow the flow of water. Ask students to think of different ways this might be accomplished. Some ideas might include using fences, plants, trees, and dams. Encourage students to build their own models and test various methods to control erosion. This can be accomplished using water, large pans, sand, soil, gravel, small rocks, and twigs or other small items to simulate trees, dams, and fences. First, student groups create a barren landscape, with a hill or mountain of sand and soil placed at one end of their pan. They can use a spray bottle to simulate rain or pour water gently down their hill and make observations. Does the soil run into the water? How much is left behind? How much does it change the color of the water? What effect might this have on wildlife in and around the environment? Students should remove the excess water from the pan and rebuild the mountain or hill at the end. This time, student groups can add twigs, rocks, gravel, and other items to try to hold the soil in place. Teams can apply water again and observe the changes. Students can perfect their erosion control model, and then each group can demonstrate how they used various materials and designs to minimize erosion in their landscape. Once they have finished, have students find real-life examples of erosion and erosion control on the school grounds, in their community, and around their homes.

11 Earth Science

Activity 94. Monitoring Weather in the Schoolyard (preK–8)

NSES Science Content Standards

- Unifying concepts and processes in science
- Science as inquiry
- Life science
- Earth and space science
- Science and technology
- Science in personal and social perspectives

Students generally love to keep a daily record of data such as seedling growth, rates of diffusion, and weather conditions. This easy project can be set up in the schoolyard, so students can monitor conditions all year.

a. Making a schoolyard weather station (preK–8)

Although commercially constructed weather stations can be purchased from science supply houses, making an affordable weather station that provides basic weather conditions is not difficult or expensive. Rainfall, for example, can be measured with a simple rain gauge made from a large soup can. Using this instrument, rainfall can be calculated in inches by measuring the amount of water collected in the can during the storm (from the time the rain begins to the time it ends). Evaporation rate, another weather condition, can be figured using the same soup can setup. Students pour water into the can to a specific line early in the day; at end of the day, they add water to the can to bring the water level back up to the line. The amount of water needed to reach the line will provide a record of the amount of evaporation during the hours between measurements. If you let the students determine the units on the makeshift instruments, the station will spark even more interest. Other instruments that can be used at a weather station are a nonmercury thermometer, which will provide a fairly accurate measure of temperature, and a wet-bulb/dry-bulb thermometer to measure relative humidity. Students can easily make a wet-bulb/dry-bulb thermometer using two standard thermometers taped side by side. To make the wet bulb, wrap a small piece of gauze around the recording end of one thermometer and saturate the gauze with water. The recording end of the second thermometer should be left dry. Place the two thermometers in the Sun for about 15 minutes and read the temperature differences. Repeatedly swinging the two thermometers in a large arc will speed up the process. Sunrise and sunset times can be found in the local newspaper, and wind direction can be identified with streamers of crepe paper. The streamers and Beauford scale listed on page 117 can be used to determine wind speed.

Topic: How Can
Weather Be Predicted?
Go to: www.scilinks.org
Code: SYS044

Table 11.1

Beauford Scale of Wind

This scale lists everyday features to help students predict the speed of the wind.

Beauford #	mph	Wind Description	Specifications
0	less than 1	Calm	Calm; smoke rises vertically
1	1–3	Light air	Direction of wind shown by smoke drift
2	4–7	Light breeze	Wind felt on face; leaves rustle
3	8–12	Gentle breeze	Leaves and small twigs in constant motion
4	13–18	Moderate breeze	Raises dust; small branches move
5	19–24	Fresh breeze	Small trees in leaf sway; waves crest on water
6	25–31	Strong breeze	Large branches in motion; umbrella use difficult
7	32–38	Moderate gale	Whole trees in motion; difficulty walking into wind
8	39–46	Fresh gale	Twigs break off trees; walking into wind impeded
9	47–53	Strong gale	Slight structural damage (shingles pulled off roof)
10	55–63	Whole gale	Trees uprooted; considerable structural damage
11	64–72	Storm	Widespread property damage occurs
12	73 and above	Hurricane	Structural damage and destruction

b. Making a rain gauge out of a soda bottle (preK–8)

This easy-to-make gauge requires a student to carefully use scissors or a knife to cut the top off an empty, clean 2 L soda bottle at the point where the bottle narrows to the cap. Invert the cut section into the bottle to act as a funnel so water is directed cleanly into the vessel. After a rain, the depth of water collected in the bottle can be measured with a ruler (as inches of rain). If students are interested in the volume of water collected, they can use a graduated cylinder from a commercial supplier or figure the volume collected by applying the following formula: depth of rain collected × area of the funnel opening = volume of rain water.

c. Judging wind direction through kite flying (preK–8)

Most students enjoy constructing their own kite. Although there are dozens of ways to make a kite, one of the easiest is to find two lightweight sticks of different lengths and lash them tightly together with twine so the shorter stick is perpendicular to the longer (in the shape of a cross). To secure the lashing, students place a spot of glue over the twine where the two sticks cross. Students can cut a shallow notch at the ends of the sticks and run a length of twine tightly around the cross. As they frame the sticks, students should make a small loop at the top and bottom of the cross. The string frame must be taut, but not so tight that the frame is warped. Students then use a sheet of cloth or paper fitted across the frame, allowing an inch of

excess, which will be folded around the string and glued or taped securely so the material is tight. Next, students cut another piece of string, which will loosely connect the loop at the top of the kite with the loop at the bottom. Before tying this string to the loops, students form a small loop in this string about two-thirds of the way between the bottom and the top (just above the intersection of the two framing sticks). This loop will secure the kite to the long string that runs to the ground. Students can make a tail for their kite by hanging another foot or two of the framing material to the bottom of the kite. Once the kite is in the air, students can record wind direction and estimate the wind speed, again referring to the Beauford Scale table on page 117.

Activity 95. Building Your Own Watershed (preK–8)

NSES Science Content Standards

- Unifying concepts and processes in science
- Science as inquiry
- Life science
- Earth and space science
- Science and technology
- Science in personal and social perspectives
- History and nature of science

Additional materials: newspaper, food coloring, spray bottles, white garbage bags

Topic: Watersheds
Go to: www.scilinks.org
Code: SYS045

Students should have a large open area on the school grounds for this messy activity. Team members will need newspaper, water, food coloring, spray bottles, and white garbage bags cut open. (Other colors do not allow students to see the flow patterns as clearly.) Each group wads up several sheets of newspaper, one sheet at a time, and throws them into a pile on the ground. Once they have a nice-size pile of papers, students place their piece of white plastic over the pile, covering it completely. Select students in each group to represent rainfall and local pollution sources such as mines, farms, logging sites, or factories.

Students who create rainfall should have clear water in their spray bottles, while those who represent pollution should have different-color water, such as red, blue, or green. Students start spraying the plastic with water, which settles into the bumps and hollows, forming rivers, streams, and lakes that are clearly defined. At this point, students draw a map of their watershed, indicating where major features are located. Challenge them to predict what they expect to see if a pollution source is located at a given area. Encourage them to introduce a pollutant to see what happens. Let them introduce another pollutant in a different location and follow the same procedure. They can demonstrate point pollution by spraying in a single location, or widespread pollution by spraying over the entire model to see where the colored water collects.

Once they have explored these point sources, students can introduce another spray bottle with a nonpoint source pollutant. This might have yellow food coloring to represent acid rain, for example. Encourage students to spray this colored water over the entire watershed and see what happens again. Once students have experimented with the various pollutants, have them spray clear water again to see how much of the contamination can be cleared up if no additional pollution is introduced. Encourage teams to record their findings in their nature journals. Among the items they have recorded, students should note whether the watershed returns to its original condition (and why or why not). Ask students to write a journal entry explaining how this activity relates to their own watershed.

Activity 96. Getting to Know the Rock Cycle (4–8)

NSES Science Content Standards

- Unifying concepts and processes in science
- Physical science
- Earth and space science

SCI**LINKS**.
THE WORLD'S A CLICK AWAY

Topic: Rock Cycle
Go to: *www.scilinks.org*
Code: SYS046

Students are surprised to learn that much of nature exists in cycles. Young students learn about the water cycle in first or second grade, and older students learn that basic elements such as nitrogen, oxygen, and carbon are repeatedly recycled. Despite this, many students are surprised to learn that rock types are also part of a cycle. Igneous rock can change into sedimentary or metamorphic rock. Sedimentary rock can change into metamorphic or igneous rock. Metamorphic rock can change into igneous or sedimentary rock.

Igneous rock forms when lava or magma, the melted rock that spills out of volcanoes, cools and hardens. Magma is made of melted minerals, and when cooled (either above or below the ground), it forms crystals. Water and wind work on the crystalline rock, eroding it into tiny fragments that can be transported to other locations. These small sediments can collect and become cemented together, forming what we call sedimentary rock. As the small fragments pile on top of each other, pressure on the fragments becomes greater and greater. Accompanying the pressure is heat produced from friction between particles, the sliding of rocks over each other (faulting) and the Earth itself. The pressure and heat combine to bake the mass into another form called metamorphic rock. There is no prescribed sequence to the rock cycle; rocks are formed by other rocks, and a rock may take more than one path through the rock cycle. For example, sedimentary rock can be weathered, eroded, and turned into sediments. It can also be melted and turned into an igneous rock.

Students try to locate examples of each rock form around the schoolyard. As teams search, they should look for particular clues in the features of the rocks. Sedimentary rock is generally soft and breaks apart or crumbles easily. Close examination of sedimentary rock also may reveal sand, pebbles, and even fossil fragments through the rock. In metamorphic rock, students can often see ribbonlike patterns and crystals formed by the growth of specific minerals within the rock. In igneous rock, students will not find crystals, but sometimes they can find holes left by gas bubbles trapped when the rock cooled. Also, the surface of igneous rock often looks shiny and glasslike because of its quick transformation from lava to rock.

Activity 97. Comparing Pebbles, Stones, and Rocks (preK–8)

NSES Science Content Standards

- Unifying concepts and processes in science
- Science as inquiry
- Earth and space science

Topic: Types of Rocks
Go to: www.scilinks.org
Code: SYS047

Students can become interested in rock studies by simply collecting a number of different-size rocks. A great challenge for younger students is to try to find one rock type in each of the categories. Ranging from smallest to largest, the rock sizes are speck (tiny flake of dirt), dust (fine powder), grain (pinpoint), sand (flattened pinhead), pebble (large, rounded pinhead), stone (fingertip, marble), rock (fist), and boulder (Volkswagen bug).

- *Finding pebbles and stones of different colors:* People tend not to notice the huge variety of colors seen in pebbles and stones. Children can find more than a dozen different colors when they apply themselves to this effort. Challenge teams to find 10, 12, or whatever number of different-color pebbles is appropriate for the class.

- *Finding pebbles and stones that have different patterns or designs:* As with colors, patterns on rocks and pebbles vary. To develop students' interest and observational skills, challenge students to find 10 pebbles that have different surface patterns.

- *Finding pebbles and stones with different surface textures:* The natural history of a pebble or stone influences the character of its surface. Round, smooth surfaces generally indicate a history of erosive sedimentation, while rough, jagged surfaces tend to suggest recent dislodgement from a larger boulder. Children have a harder time distinguishing minor variations in surface roughness compared to patterns or colors in rocks, so make the goal of this activity less structured.

Activity 98. Identifying Types of Minerals and Rocks (4–8)

NSES Science Content Standards

- Unifying concepts and processes in science
- Science as inquiry
- Earth and space science

What is the difference between rocks and minerals? Minerals are naturally occurring homogeneous solids, meaning that they are the same all the way through. Rocks are naturally occurring solid aggregates, which means that they are generally made up of two or more minerals. Many combinations of minerals can make up a rock, and because there are more than 3,000 known minerals, there are exponentially more rock types.

Experts suggest students who want to learn how to identify the various kinds of rocks look at individual rocks and minerals as often as possible to become familiar with them. Many books can help with identification, and many sites on the internet contain excellent photographs of various specimens.

Rock features that are easiest to find include different colors of the surface, how the rock breaks (called its cleavage pattern), the surface luster (the way it looks in the light), different crystal shapes within the rock, whether the rock shows magnetic qualities (iron), the different weights of similar-size rocks (density), and whether the rock can be scratched easily. Working in teams, have students collect at least five rocks in the schoolyard that demonstrate these features.

Some of the most common colors are golden yellow (pyrite), bronze (nickel), copper-red (copper), silver yellow (silver), and rainbow (bornite). The rock may not have a particular color (barite), or it may be dirty white (gypsum or quartz), yellow-brown (jasper or sulfur), turquoise green (amazonite or feldspar), blue (azurite or celestite), purple or violet (amethyst or dolomite), or black or gray (titanite or hornblende).

Alternatively, luster can easily be used to help identify a mineral. Some of the most common descriptions are dull/earthy (kalolinite), waxy (opal, chalcedony), greasy (nepheine), pearly (talc, muscovite), silky (gypsum, kernite), glassy (quartz, obsidian), resinous or brilliant (sphalerite), and metallic (hematite, pyrite).

Another characteristic that can be used is density (specific gravity). Specific gravity is how many times more than an equal amount of water the material weighs. This is a good way to identify the minerals if each rock used in the exercise is the same size. Examples include very light (borax), light (gypsum or halite), average (calcite, feldspar, or quartz), slightly heavy (biotite mica), heavy (hematite, nickel, or iron), extremely heavy (gold or silver), and terribly heavy (platinum).

Cleavage is another way to identify rocks. This characteristic denotes how a rock will break and is usually described as perfect, good, imperfect, or poor.

One common way to classify rocks is by determining hardness. Examples of this feature include crumbles (talc), very soft and can be scratched with a fingernail (gypsum), soft and can be scratched with a penny (calcite), semisoft and can be scratched with a thorn (fluorite), hard and can be scratched with a nail (apatite), semihard and can barely scratch glass (feldspar), hard and can be scratched with a concrete nail (quartz or topaz), very hard and is used to cut and grind (corundum), and extremely hard (diamond).

Activity 99. Telling Time With a Sundial (4–8)

NSES Science Content Standards

- Unifying concepts and processes in science
- Science as inquiry
- Life science
- Earth and space science
- Science and technology
- Science in personal and social perspectives
- History and nature of science

Additional materials: compass, smooth material (e.g., coffee can lid, small wooden disk), straight rod (e.g., nail, post, stick)

Students are often surprised by how accurate sundials can be. A simple sundial consists of a large circle on any smooth material (from a coffee can lid to a circle drawn in the sand), a sunny day, and a compass for accurately finding north. Small wooden disks (such as checkers) or "tree cookies" (thin slices from a 2–3 in. diameter tree branch) work especially well; students can drill a small hole for string in these disks opposite the marking for north to make key chains or necklaces. This way they can try the sundials in different locations or easily transport them home to test at times when they aren't in school. Students place numbers or marks around the circle (as in a clock) and position the 12 o'clock mark to point north. At the center of the circle, students drive a straight rod appropriate for the size of the sundial face (nail, post, or stick) into the ground, tilt or bend it toward north at the same angle (find this angle by using a protractor) as the school's latitude, and watch where the shadow falls. For example, a school located at 40°N latitude would need the nail or stick bent to a 40-degree angle. The shadow will be on the standard time for your location. If a compass is not available and you know the current time, point the shadow of the rod to that hour and the sundial will show you north (also an effective means of finding your way if you are lost).

Activity 100. Our Solar System (preK–8)

NSES Science Content Standards

- Unifying concepts and processes in science
- Science as inquiry
- Life science
- Earth and space science
- Science and technology
- Science in personal and social perspectives
- History and nature of science

Astronomy is probably the oldest science known to mankind, and stargazing is one of the earliest hobbies. When students learn about astronomy, plan an evening or two when students return to the schoolyard after the Sun goes down. Plan the event soon after the dinner hour, and invite parents to take part in the adventure. Alternatively, hold a sky gazing night for the students on the same evening their parents come to the school to meet the teachers. This requires someone other than the teacher to lead the night sky activities. Older students who attend the school and have previously attended one of these events evening are generally willing volunteers. Many of the following activities can be done the day after the evening meeting. Students should also be reminded to dress warmly, as it is often chillier in the evening than during the day.

Stargazing is improved when using binoculars or a telescope to look at stars, planets, and the Moon. Enhanced magnification not only brings out the features of bodies such as the Moon and planets but also reveals the magnificent star fields of the Milky Way. Participants generally find that larger binoculars are better than smaller ones because more light is gathered by the lenses. *Remind students never to look at the Sun with binoculars or a telescope.*

a. About planets (preK–8)

Many students know that Earth is a planet, and some know our solar system holds seven more (Mercury, Venus, Mars, Jupiter, Saturn, Uranus, and Neptune). Pluto is also included here, although it is no longer recognized as a planet. Furthermore, it is possible to see the five brightest planets in the sky with or without binoculars. The five planets easiest to see are Mercury, Venus, Mars, Jupiter, and Saturn. Most remarkable is that each planet has its own characteristics. Mercury and Venus (the inner planets), for example, are always found near the Sun, and therefore they are visible just after sunset or just before sunrise. In addition, Venus is the brightest planet, while Mercury is so close to the Sun that it can be seen only at twilight. Mars can best be seen when it is on the opposite side of the Earth from the Sun and at its brightest stage. Jupiter and Saturn are less pronounced but also largest and brightest when they are on the opposite side the Earth. Four of the five planets can also be distinguished by color. Mars is red, Saturn is yellow, Jupiter is blue, and Venus is white. Unfortunately, the characteristics of Uranus, Neptune, and Pluto are not discernable without powerful magnification.

Some experts note that planets can be distinguished from stars because they do not appear to twinkle, so students should be able to pick them out in the sky. In addition, planets emerge sooner than stars in the evening and are frequently seen at daybreak. Although the planetary timeline does not fit perfectly in our year, students should be able to find the planets at various times during the year, as listed on page 124. Challenge students to spot as many planets as they can in the evening or morning sky.

January: Mercury, Jupiter, and Venus in the morning

February: Venus, Jupiter, and Mercury in the morning

March: Venus, Saturn, Jupiter, Mercury, and Mars in the morning

April: Mercury, Saturn, Venus, Jupiter, and Mars in the morning

May: Mercury, Saturn, Jupiter, Neptune, Venus, and Mars in the morning

June: Jupiter, Venus, Mars, and Mercury in the morning

July: Jupiter, Venus, and Mars in the morning

August: Jupiter in the morning; Saturn in the evening

September: Jupiter, Venus, and Mars in the morning; Saturn and Mercury in the evening

October: Jupiter in the evening

November: Saturn and Venus in the morning; Jupiter and Mars in the evening

December: Venus in the morning; Mars and Saturn in the evening

b. About the Moon (preK–8)

One of the most obvious objects the students will see in the sky above the school grounds is the Moon. This object is the closest celestial body to the Earth and rotates around us every 24 hours. The Moon is also smaller and less dense than the Earth and creates only $\frac{1}{6}$ of the gravitational force that the Earth creates. Furthermore, the crust of the Moon is thinner than the Earth's crust, and its surface shows the effects of an incredibly high number of meteorite bombardments.

From our vantage point, the Moon is the brightest object in the evening sky, yet it does not produce its own light. Instead, it appears luminescent because it reflects sunlight. The Moon also goes through a series of phases during the month; during this time it goes from full Moon to waning gibbous to last quarter to waning crescent to new (dark) Moon to waxing crescent to first quarter to waxing gibbous and finally full again. We know, however, that the Moon does not change its shape over the entire period. Challenge students to come up with an explanation for why the Moon looks different in its various phases.

Activity 101. The Universe (preK–8)

NSES Science Content Standards

- Unifying concepts and processes in science
- Science as inquiry
- Physical science
- Earth and space science
- Science and technology
- Science in personal and social perspectives
- History and nature of science

Once students have looked at the Moon and planets that make up our solar system, they can look at stars and other bodies farther away. Students have a hard time comprehending the distances involved, but they will be able to spot several important stars and constellations and will also see meteors if they are patient.

SCI LINKS®
THE WORLD'S A CLICK AWAY

Topic: Solar System Formation
Go to: *www.scilinks.org*
Code: SYS050

a. About stars (4–8)

The heavens are full of stars; students can just look into the sky on a clear night and be convinced of this. Many students do not realize that the stars move in the sky. Because of the rotation of the Earth, stars in the western sky are seen for only a short period of time, while stars that rise in the east will appear to move across the sky toward the west. It is more difficult for students to understand the vast amount of distance between the billions of stars in the heavens and that these stars make up our galaxy. In addition, most students know that our Sun is really a star and that it constantly emits a huge amount of energy. Challenge teams to think about the various types of energy that a star gives off. Using the Sun as an example, ask teams to come up with five different types of energy.

> The types of energy coming off the Sun as different-length waves are referred to as the electromagnetic spectrum. Starting with the shortest wavelength (in a condensed list), they are gamma rays, x-rays, ultraviolet rays, light rays, infrared rays, microwaves, and radio waves.

b. About constellations (preK–8)

Constellations are groupings of stars naturally arranged to suggest specific figures. There are 88 different constellations in the heavens, some of which are never seen by viewers in the northern or southern hemisphere, despite the Earth's tilt. To view constellations in the northern hemisphere, beginners should start by finding one of the brightest groups of stars in the north. This constellation, the third largest in the sky, is known as the Big Dipper (Ursa Major); keep in mind that the Big Dipper is not always right-side-up. Locate the basin and handle of the constellation and find the two stars that form the pouring edge of the Big Dipper's bowl (on the side away from the handle). These two stars point directly at the North Star, a semibright star known as Polaris, located at the end of the handle of the Little Dipper (Ursa Minor). The handle and bowl of Ursa Minor rotate around Polaris every 24 hours so the little dipper is never in the same position when viewed at different times on the same night. If students continue the line past Polaris about as far as they traveled from the Big Dipper to the North Star, they will come to the constellation, Cassiopeia, the Queen of Ethiopia. This constellation is formed by a *W*-shape series of stars so it appears that the Queen is reclining in the Milky Way. Returning to the North Star, students can carefully scan the sky to the right, the left, above, and below the Little Dipper to locate more bright stars in specific constellations. It is always helpful for beginners to have a star wheel (planisphere) handy to help identify stars and constellations in the evening sky. The Big Dipper, Cassiopeia, and Little Dipper are visible year-round in the Northern Hemisphere, but most of the constellations can be seen only at certain times of the year. Challenge members of each team to locate Cassiopeia, Ursa Major, Ursa Minor, and the North Star with their binoculars.

c. About meteors (4–8)

Stars are not the only things students can see when they look into the night sky. On a clear night, students will likely see streaks of light dart across the sky. These are *meteors*, boulder-size rocks that become caught in the Earth's gravity and are drawn through the atmosphere toward the ground. Fortunately, in the process the meteors heat to more than 3000°F and disintegrate due to the friction with atmospheric particles. Periodically, however, a few may reach the ground before they burn up entirely; meteors that reach the ground are called *meteorites*. Challenge teams to come up with three logical sources in outer space for these rocky masses.

Some meteors are bits broken off asteroids, a belt of rocky debris orbiting the Sun between Mars and Jupiter. Others are rocky chunks that are thrown high into the heavens from a meteorite impact with the Moon or another planet. Others are dust particles coming off the tails of comets.

Resources

Carle, E. 2009. *The tiny seed.* New York: Little Simon.

Colburn, A., and M. Clough. 1997. Implementing the learning cycle. *The Science Teacher* 64 (5): 30–33.

Collette, A., and E. Chiappetta. 1994. *Science instruction in the middle and secondary schools.* New York: Macmillan.

Davies, M. A., and M. Wavering. 1999. Alternative assessment: New directions in teaching and learning. *Contemporary Education* 71 (1): 39–45.

Deming, J., and M. Cracolice. 2004. Learning how to think. *The Science Teacher* 71 (3): 42–47.

Dorros, A. 1986. *Ant cities.* New York: HarperCollins.

Duran, L. 2003. Investigating brine shrimp. *Science Activities* 40 (2): 30–34.

Eisenkraft, A. 2003. Expanding the 5E model. *The Science Teacher* 70 (6): 56–59.

Himmelman, J. 1999. *A dandelion's life.* Danbury, CT: Children's Press.

Krantz, P. 2004. Inquiry, slime, and the national standards. *Science Activities* 41 (3): 22–25.

Lawson, A. 1988. A better way to teach biology. *The American Biology Teacher* 50 (5): 266–273.

Lawson, A. 2001. Using the learning cycle to teach biology concepts and reasoning patterns. *Journal of Biological Education* 35 (4): 165–169.

National Research Council (NRC). 1996. *National science education standards.* Washington, DC: National Academies Press.

O'Brien, T., and D. Seager. 2000. 5 E(z) steps to teaching Earth-Moon scaling: An interdisciplinary mathematics/science/technology mini-unit. *School Science and Mathematics* 100 (7): 390–395.

Odom, A., and P. Kelly. 1998. Making learning meaningful. *The Science Teacher* 65 (4): 33–37.

Rillero, P. 1999. Raphanus sativus, germination and inquiry: A learning cycle approach for novice experimenters. *Electronic Journal of Science Education* 3 (4). (ERIC Document Reproduction Service No. EJ651190)

Trowbridge, L., and R. Bybee. 1990. *Becoming a secondary school science teacher.* 5th ed. Englewood Cliffs, NJ: Merrill.

Volkmann, M., and S. Abell. 2003. Seamless assessment. *Science and Children* 40 (8): 41–5.

Wilder, M., and P. Shuttleworth. 2005. Cell inquiry: A 5E learning cycle lesson. *Science Activities* 41 (4): 36–43.

Content Resources

Note: This list is far from complete! This is just designed to give teachers a place to start. Individual backgrounds and local resources will vary, and teachers will find appropriate resources more easily as they become familiar with their schoolyard.

Field Guides

- Audubon Field Guide series (Chanticleer Press, New York)
- Golden Field Guide series (Golden Press, New York)
- Peterson Field Guide series (Houghton Mifflin, Boston and New York)
- Simon & Schuster Nature Guide series (Simon & Schuster, New York)

Identification Websites

- Cornell Lab of Ornithology (birds): *www.birds.cornell.edu/netcommunity/Page.aspx?pid=1478*
- eNature (all types of organisms): *www.enature.com/home*
- Insect Identification.org (insects): *www.insectidentification.org*
- My Plant ID (plants): *www.myplantid.com*
- NCSU Turffiles Broadleaf Identification (plants): *www.turffiles.ncsu.edu/turfid/ItemID.aspx?orderID=BL&orderDesc=Broadleaf*
- Wildflower Identification (wildflowers): *www.realtimerendering.com/flowers/flowers.html*
- What Tree Is It? (tree): *www.oplin.org/tree*

Government Websites

- Invasive Species: *www.invasivespeciesinfo.gov*
- Science.gov (links to all types of information): *www.science.gov/browse/w_115.htm*
- USDA Plants: *http://plants.usda.gov*
- U.S. Fish and Wildlife Service: *www.fws.gov*

Organizations

Guest speakers, samples, and background information may be available through these resources.

- County extension offices
- National, state, and local park offices
- Area colleges and universities
- Audubon societies
- State and local conservation offices
- Watershed groups
- State and local fish and wildlife offices

Index